ClearRevise®

AQA GCSE
Physical Education 8582

Illustrated revision and practice

Published by
PG Online Limited
The Old Coach House
35 Main Road
Tolpuddle
Dorset
DT2 7EW
United Kingdom

sales@pgonline.co.uk
www.clearrevise.com
www.pgonline.co.uk
2023

PG ONLINE

PREFACE

Absolute clarity! That's the aim.

This is everything you need to ace your exams and beam with pride. Each topic is laid out in a beautifully illustrated format that is clear, approachable and as concise and simple as possible. Each section of the specification is clearly indicated to help you cross-reference your revision. The checklist on the contents pages will help you keep track of what you have already worked through and what's left before the big day.

We have included worked exam-style questions with answers. There is also a set of exam-style questions at the end of each section for you to practise writing responses. You can check your answers against those given at the end of the book.

ACKNOWLEDGMENTS

The questions in this ClearRevise guide are the sole responsibility of the authors and have neither been provided nor approved by the examination board.

Every effort has been made to trace and acknowledge ownership of copyright. The publishers will be happy to make any future amendments with copyright owners that it has not been possible to contact. The publisher would like to thank the following companies and individuals who granted permission for the use of their images in this textbook.

Longjumper © Stefan Holm / Shutterstock.com
Basketball game © Pavel Shchegolev / Shutterstock.com
Pommel horse routine © Michele Morrone / Shutterstock.com
Nathon Allen © Simon Balson / Alamy Stock Photo
Throw-in © katatonia82 / Shutterstock.com
Long jump take-off © John Bingham / Alamy Stock Photo
Kayak sprint © Celso Pupo / Shutterstock.com
Javelin thrower © Shahjehan / Shutterstock.com
Rugby match © Mai Groves / Shutterstock.com
Cross country jump © Anthony Delgado / Shutterstock.com
London Marathon © IR Stone / Shutterstock.com
Boxing match © Dmitry Niko / Shutterstock.com
Trampoline practice © Erin Deleon / Shutterstock
AJ MacGinty © Action Plus Sports Images / Alamy Stock Photo
Nafissatou Thiam © SPP Sport Press Photo. / Alamy Stock Photo
Hunter Armstrong © Aflo Co. Ltd. / Alamy Stock Photo
Rugby tackle © News Images LTD / Alamy Stock Photo
Rachel Daly © Jose Breton- Pics Action / Shutterstock.com
Pattaya Tadtong © FocusDzign / Shutterstock.com
Camera operator © Paolo Bona / Shutterstock.com
Sponsorship boards © Jordan Tan / Shutterstock.com
England Women's Rugby Team © atsportphoto / Shutterstock.com
Rolex store © Dr. Victor Wong / Shutterstock.com
Mo Farah, London © Matthew Pull / Shutterstock.com
Stefanos Tsitsipas © Alex Bogatyrev / Shutterstock.com
England Men's Rugby Team © Marco Iacobucci Epp / Shutterstock.com
Emirates Stadium © gowithstock / Shutterstock.com
Rory McIlroy © Gary Yee / Shutterstock.com

England Women's Football © Influential Photography / Shutterstock.com
FIFA referee © Saolab Press / Shutterstock.com
Aquatics Centre, London © Ron Ellis / Shutterstock.com
VAR review © ph.FAB / Shutterstock.com
Sponsored screen © katatonia82 / Shutterstock.com
Nick Kyrgios © Rena Schild / Shutterstock.com
VAR signal © RedCap / Shutterstock.com
British newspapers © Lenscap Photography / Shutterstock.com
Rugby handshake © Oleksandr Osipov / Shutterstock.com
Reaction to line judge © Alex Bogatyrev / Shutterstock.com
Olympic athletes © Action Plus Sports Images / Alamy Stock Photo
Discus throw © Shahjehan / Shutterstock.com
World Boxing Championships match © Paolo Bona / Shutterstock.com
Road cyclists © Paul Higley / Shutterstock.com
Marissa Papacostantinou © Avpics / Alamy Stock Photo
Marion Jones © Allstar Picture Library / Alamy Stock Photo
Jong Su Kim © Adam Pretty / Staff
Adrian Mutu © ph.FAB / Shutterstock.com
Football spectators © Clive Chilvers / Shutterstock.com
Litter after match © alberto_girotto / Shutterstock.com
Marseille spectator clash © alberto_girotto / Shutterstock.com
Marseille spectator injury © alberto_girotto / Shutterstock.com
Shot put athlete © EvrenKalinbacak / Shutterstock.com
Adam Peaty © Salty View / Shutterstock
Rose Harvey © PA Images / Alamy Stock Photo
Anthonique Strachan © PA Images / Alamy Stock Photo
Chris Froome © Radu Razvan / Shutterstock.com

Design and artwork: Jessica Webb / PG Online Ltd

First edition 2023   10 9 8 7 6 5 4 3 2
A catalogue entry for this book is available from the British Library
ISBN: 978-1-916518-04-9
With contributions from R Howitt
Copyright © PG Online 2023
All rights reserved

This product is made of material from well-managed FSC® certified forests and from recycled materials.

Printed by Bell & Bain Ltd, Glasgow, UK.

MIX
Paper | Supporting
responsible forestry
FSC® C007785

THE SCIENCE OF REVISION

Illustrations and words

Research has shown that revising with words and pictures doubles the quality of responses by students.[1] This is known as 'dual-coding' because it provides two ways of fetching the information from our brain. The improvement in responses is particularly apparent in students when they are asked to apply their knowledge to different problems. Recall, application and judgement are all specifically and carefully assessed in public examination questions.

Retrieval of information

Retrieval practice encourages students to come up with answers to questions.[2] The closer the question is to one you might see in a real examination, the better. Also, the closer the environment in which a student revises is to the 'examination environment', the better. Students who had a test 2–7 days away did 30% better using retrieval practice than students who simply read, or repeatedly reread material. Students who were expected to teach the content to someone else after their revision period did better still.[3] What was found to be most interesting in other studies is that students using retrieval methods and testing for revision were also more resilient to the introduction of stress.[4]

Ebbinghaus' forgetting curve and spaced learning

Ebbinghaus' 140-year-old study examined the rate at which we forget things over time. The findings still hold true. However, the act of forgetting facts and techniques and relearning them is what cements them into the brain.[5] Spacing out revision is more effective than cramming – we know that, but students should also know that the space between revisiting material should vary depending on how far away the examination is. A cyclical approach is required. An examination 12 months away necessitates revisiting covered material about once a month. A test in 30 days should have topics revisited every 3 days – intervals of roughly a tenth of the time available.[6]

Summary

Students: the more tests and past questions you do, in an environment as close to examination conditions as possible, the better you are likely to perform on the day. If you prefer to listen to music while you revise, tunes without lyrics will be far less detrimental to your memory and retention. Silence is most effective.[5] If you choose to study with friends, choose carefully – effort is contagious.[7]

1. Mayer, R. E., & Anderson, R. B. (1991). Animations need narrations: An experimental test of dual-coding hypothesis. *Journal of Education Psychology*, (83)4, 484–490.

2. Roediger III, H. L., & Karpicke, J.D. (2006). Test-enhanced learning: Taking memory tests improves long-term retention. *Psychological Science*, 17(3), 249–255.

3. Nestojko, J., Bui, D., Kornell, N. & Bjork, E. (2014). Expecting to teach enhances learning and organisation of knowledge in free recall of text passages. *Memory and Cognition*, 42(7), 1038–1048.

4. Smith, A. M., Floerke, V. A., & Thomas, A. K. (2016) Retrieval practice protects memory against acute stress. *Science*, 354(6315), 1046–1048.

5. Perham, N., & Currie, H. (2014). Does listening to preferred music improve comprehension performance? *Applied Cognitive Psychology*, 28(2), 279–284.

6. Cepeda, N. J., Vul, E., Rohrer, D., Wixted, J. T. & Pashler, H. (2008). Spacing effects in learning a temporal ridgeline of optimal retention. *Psychological Science*, 19(11), 1095–1102.

7. Busch, B. & Watson, E. (2019), *The Science of Learning*, 1st ed. Routledge.

CONTENTS

Paper 1

Topic 1   Applied anatomy and physiology

Specification point			☑
3.1.1.1	Bones	2	☐
3.1.1.1	Structure and functions of the skeleton	3	☐
3.1.1.1	Muscles and joints	4	☐
3.1.1.1	How joints differ in design to allow certain types of movement	6	☐
3.1.1.1	How the major muscles and muscle groups of the body work	7	☐
3.1.1.2	The lungs and gas exchange	8	☐
3.1.1.2	Blood vessels	9	☐
3.1.1.2	Structure of the heart	10	☐
3.1.1.2	Cardiac output, stroke volume and heart rate	11	☐
3.1.1.2	Mechanics of breathing	12	☐
3.1.1.2	Interpretation of a spirometer trace	13	☐
3.1.1.3	Aerobic and anaerobic exercise	14	☐
3.1.1.3	Excess post-exercise oxygen	15	☐
3.1.1.3	The short- and long-term effects of exercise	16	☐
	Examination practice 1	**18**	☐

Topic 2   Movement analysis

Specification point			☑
3.1.2.1	Lever systems	20	☐
3.1.2.1	Mechanical advantage	22	☐
3.1.2.1	Analysis of basic upper-body movements in sporting examples	23	☐
3.1.2.1	Analysis of basic lower-body movements in sporting examples	25	☐
3.1.2.2	Planes and axis of movement	26	☐
	Examination practice 2	**28**	☐

Topic 3   Physical training

Specification point			☑
3.1.3.1	Health and fitness	29	☐
3.1.3.2	The components of fitness	30	☐
3.1.3.2	Measuring the components of fitness	32	☐
3.1.3.2	Demonstration of how data is collected for fitness testing	37	☐
3.1.3.3	The principles of training and overload	38	☐
3.1.3.3	Types of training	39	☐
3.1.3.4	Calculating intensities to optimise training effectiveness	44	☐
3.1.3.4	Considerations to prevent injury	46	☐

3.1.3.4	High altitude training	47 ☐
3.1.3.4	Seasonal aspects of training	48 ☐
3.1.3.5	Effective use of warm up and cool down	49 ☐
	Examination practice 3	**50** ☐

Topic 4   Use of data

Specification point ☑

3.1.4.1	Understanding how data is collected	52 ☐
3.1.4.2	Presenting data	53 ☐
3.1.4.3	Analysis and evaluation of data	54 ☐
	Examination practice 4	**56** ☐

Paper 2

Topic 1   Sports psychology

Specification point ☑

3.2.1.1	Classification of skills	58 ☐
3.2.1.1–2	Goal setting	59 ☐
3.2.1.2	SMART targets	60 ☐
3.2.1.3	Basic information processing	61 ☐
3.2.1.4	Guidance on performance	62 ☐
3.2.1.4	Feedback on performance	64 ☐
3.2.1.5	Arousal and the inverted-U theory	65 ☐
3.2.1.5	Using stress management techniques to control arousal levels	66 ☐
3.2.1.5	Direct and indirect aggression	67 ☐
3.2.1.5	Introverts and extroverts	68 ☐
3.2.1.5	Intrinsic and extrinsic motivation	69 ☐
	Examination practice 5	**70** ☐

Topic 2   Socio-cultural influences

Specification point ☑

3.2.2.1	Engagement patterns of different social groups	72 ☐
3.2.2.2	Commercialisation of physical activity and sport	76 ☐
3.2.2.2	Types of sponsorship and the media	77 ☐
3.2.2.2	Positive and negative impacts of sponsorship and the media	78 ☐
3.2.2.2	Positive and negative impacts of technology	80 ☐
3.2.2.3	Conduct of performers	82 ☐
3.2.2.3	Prohibited substances	83 ☐
3.2.2.3	Prohibited methods (blood doping)	84 ☐
3.2.2.3	Drugs subject to certain restrictions (beta-blockers)	85 ☐
3.2.2.3	Types of performers that may use different types of PEDs	86 ☐

3.2.2.3	The advantages and disadvantages for performers of taking PEDs	87	☐
3.2.2.3	The disadvantages to sports or events of performers taking PEDs	88	☐
3.2.2.3	Spectator behaviour	89	☐
3.2.2.3	Hooliganism	90	☐
	Examination practice 6	**92**	☐

Topic 3   Health, fitness and wellbeing

Specification point			☑
3.2.3.1	Physical, emotional and social health, fitness and wellbeing	93	☐
3.2.3.2	The consequences of a sedentary lifestyle	94	☐
3.2.3.2	Obesity and performance	95	☐
3.2.3.2	Somatotypes	96	☐
3.2.3.3	Energy use	98	☐
3.2.3.3	Diet	99	☐
3.2.3.3	Nutrition	100	☐
3.2.3.3	Reasons for maintaining water balance	101	☐
	Examination practice 7	**102**	☐

Non-exam assessment (NEA)

Practical performance in physical activity and sport

NEA element			☑
	Performance assessment: Practical performance	106	☐
	Performance analysis assessment: Analysis and evaluation	107	☐

	Examination practice answers	109	
	Levels-based mark schemes for extended response questions	117	
	Index	118	
	Examination tips	**121**	

MARK ALLOCATIONS

Green mark allocations[1] on answers to in-text questions throughout this guide help to indicate where marks are gained within the answers. A bracketed '1' e.g. [1] = one valid point worthy of a mark. In longer answer questions, a mark is given based on the whole response. In these answers, a judgement should be made using the levels-based mark scheme on page 117. There are often many more points to make than there are marks available so you have more opportunity to max out your answers than you may think.

TOPICS FOR PAPER 1
The human body and movement in physical activity and sport

Information about Paper 1

Mandatory written exam: 1 hour 15 minutes
Externally assessed.
78 marks
All questions are mandatory
30% of the qualification grade
Calculators are permitted in this examination.

Specification coverage

Applied anatomy and physiology, movement analysis, physical training, and the use of data.

The content for this assessment will be drawn from topics 3.1.1 to 3.1.4 of the specification.

Questions

The paper will consist of a mixture of multiple choice/objective test questions, short answer questions and extended answer questions.

BONES

The structure and function of the musculoskeletal system depends on the location of major bones and joints within the skeleton.

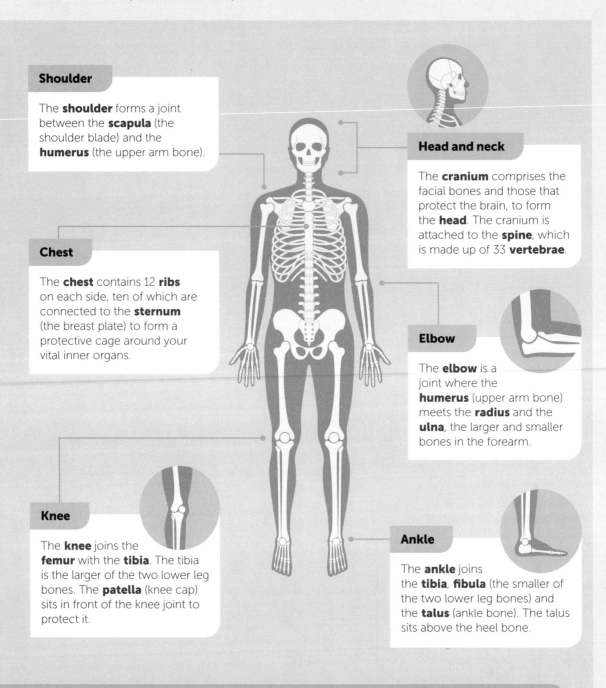

Shoulder

The **shoulder** forms a joint between the **scapula** (the shoulder blade) and the **humerus** (the upper arm bone).

Chest

The **chest** contains 12 **ribs** on each side, ten of which are connected to the **sternum** (the breast plate) to form a protective cage around your vital inner organs.

Head and neck

The **cranium** comprises the facial bones and those that protect the brain, to form the **head**. The cranium is attached to the **spine**, which is made up of 33 **vertebrae**.

Elbow

The **elbow** is a joint where the **humerus** (upper arm bone) meets the **radius** and the **ulna**, the larger and smaller bones in the forearm.

Knee

The **knee** joins the **femur** with the **tibia**. The tibia is the larger of the two lower leg bones. The **patella** (knee cap) sits in front of the knee joint to protect it.

Ankle

The **ankle** joins the **tibia**, **fibula** (the smaller of the two lower leg bones) and the **talus** (ankle bone). The talus sits above the heel bone.

Infants are born with about 270 bones in their skeleton to provide extra flexibility. During childhood, many bones fuse together ending up with typically 210 bones in the adult skeleton.

STRUCTURE AND FUNCTIONS OF THE SKELETON

The skeletal system provides a framework for movement. The muscular system attaches to the skeleton. When muscles contract, they pull the bones.

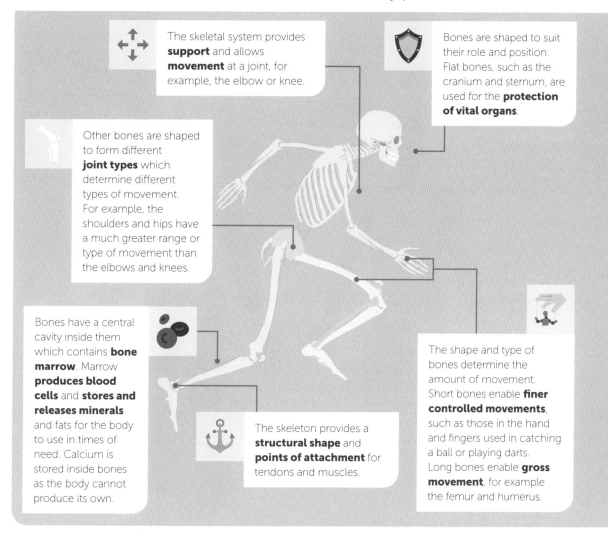

The skeletal system provides **support** and allows **movement** at a joint, for example, the elbow or knee.

Bones are shaped to suit their role and position. Flat bones, such as the cranium and sternum, are used for the **protection of vital organs**.

Other bones are shaped to form different **joint types** which determine different types of movement. For example, the shoulders and hips have a much greater range or type of movement than the elbows and knees.

Bones have a central cavity inside them which contains **bone marrow**. Marrow **produces blood cells** and **stores and releases minerals** and fats for the body to use in times of need. Calcium is stored inside bones as the body cannot produce its own.

The skeleton provides a **structural shape** and **points of attachment** for tendons and muscles.

The shape and type of bones determine the amount of movement. Short bones enable **finer controlled movements**, such as those in the hand and fingers used in catching a ball or playing darts. Long bones enable **gross movement**, for example the femur and humerus.

Anna plays rugby union.

(a) Outline **one** way in which Anna's skeleton protects her vital organs during a game of rugby. [1]

(b) Explain the role of long bones when playing a game of rugby union. [3]

(a) *Her ribs will protect her heart and lungs in a scrum or tackle.*[1]
Her skull helps to protect her brain in a tackle.[1]

(b) *More speed can be generated when running using longer levers,*[1] *which can impart a greater force / range of motion on the ball when kicking / passing.*[1] *This allows the player to pass more quickly / take longer penalty kicks to benefit gameplay.*[1]

MUSCLES AND JOINTS

There are about 600 **muscles** in the human body. **Tendons** are strong tissue used to connect muscles to bones.

Major muscles and muscle groups

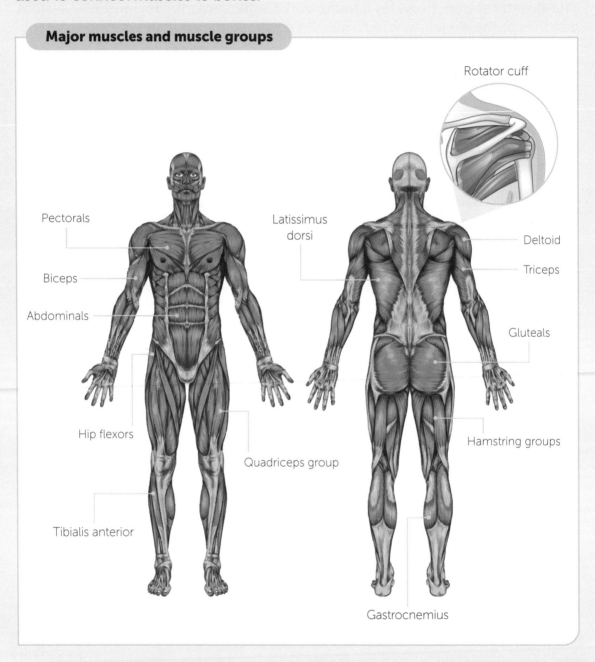

Rotator cuff

Pectorals

Latissimus dorsi

Deltoid

Triceps

Biceps

Abdominals

Gluteals

Hip flexors

Hamstring groups

Quadriceps group

Tibialis anterior

Gastrocnemius

1. Name **one** muscle group that causes movement at the knee. [1]

 1. *Hamstrings,[1] quadriceps.[1]*

Structure of a synovial joint

A   Synovial membrane

A **synovial membrane** produces and contains synovial fluid.

B   Synovial fluid

Synovial fluid lubricates a joint to help it run smoothly.

E   Cartilage

Cartilage absorbs shock and acts as a buffer between the bones.

It prevents bones from rubbing together directly, reducing wear and friction.

F-G   Ligaments / tendons

Ligaments (**F**) are flexible and elastic structures used to attach bone to bone within synovial joints. The elasticity in the ligament absorbs shock. This is contrary to **tendons** (**G**) which have less elasticity and attach bone to muscle.

C   Joint capsule

A **joint capsule** encloses and supports the joint to prevent unwanted or excessive movement..

D   Bursae

Bursae are sacs of fluid which allow bones to glide over them, helping to reduce friction.

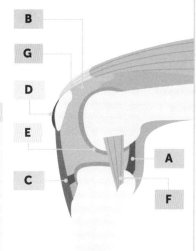

Types of freely movable joints

Hinge joints and ball and socket joints are types of synovial joints.

Hinge joints

The **elbows**, **knees** and **ankles** are example of **hinge joints**. They allow movement in one plane through flexion and extension with up to 180 degrees of motion.

Ball and socket joints

The **hips** and **shoulders** are examples of **ball and socket joints**. A ball-shaped end of one bone fits into a cup-shaped socket in another. This allows for flexion and extension, abduction and adduction, circumduction and rotational movement in almost all directions, making sporting actions such as a cricket bowl or breaststroke swimming possible.

2. David is a competitive sports performer. His shoulders, elbows and knees are in constant use.
   Describe the function of **two** synovial joint structures in the prevention of injury. [4]

   2. A synovial membrane produces and contains synovial fluid to 'oil' the joint,[1] reducing friction.[1] The joint capsule stabilises the joint[1] / distributes load around the joint and prevents wear and tear on the bone ends.[1] Bursae are soft sacs of fluid[1] that provide cushioning[1] / reduce friction by providing a surface to glide over.[1] Cartilage absorbs shock[1] and provides a buffer between bones, preventing direct friction.[1] Ligaments provide elasticity to absorb shock[1] and help keep the joint together by connecting bone to bone.[1]

HOW JOINTS DIFFER IN DESIGN TO ALLOW CERTAIN TYPES OF MOVEMENT

The following types of movement are linked to specific types of joint, which enables that movement to take place.

Flexion and extension

Flexion and **extension** occurs at the hips and shoulders, and at hinge joints such the **elbows** and **knees**, as the angle of the joint closes and opens.

Flexion in the upward phase of a bicep curl

Extension with a backhand shot in tennis

Plantar flexion and dorsiflexion

These are specialist terms for flexion and extension at the **ankle**. **Plantar flexion** means to point the toes. **Dorsiflexion** means to lift the end of the foot at the toes, pivoting at the heel.

Plantar flexion in ballet

Dorsiflexion in long jump

Abduction and adduction

Abduction and **adduction** at the shoulder means to take your arms away (to abduct) from the body, or bringing them back towards (to adduct) the midline of the body. A star jump uses both abduction and adduction.

Abduction in butterfly swimming

Adduction in pull-ups on the rings

Rotation and circumduction

Rotation of the shoulder creates a twisting of the bone along its long axis, such as when you rotate your palm up towards the sky.

Circumduction (think circumference) means a circular movement of a limb around the ball and socket joint.

The two movements are often combined.

Shoulder circumduction in canoeing

Shoulder rotation on the pommel horse

HOW THE MAJOR MUSCLES AND MUSCLE GROUPS OF THE BODY WORK

The major muscles of the body work in **antagonistic** pairs. As one muscle (**agonist**) contracts to pull a bone, the opposite muscle (**antagonist**) relaxes, to allow the bone to be pulled. This allows movements to take place and sporting actions to be executed.

Major muscles and muscle groups

Antagonistic muscle pairs at each major joint:

Shoulder: **Latissimus dorsi** and **deltoid**

Elbow: **Biceps** and **triceps**

Hip: **Hip flexors** and **gluteals**

Knee: **Hamstrings** and **quadriceps**

Ankle: **Tibialis anterior** and **gastrocnemius**

Agonists are the first muscle to start a movement (the **prime movers**). While the agonist (think pain and agony) contracts, the antagonist relaxes. The bicep may be the agonist in a pull-up, but the antagonist in a press-up.

Isometric and isotonic contractions

A **contraction** happens when a muscle is actively under load. A **concentric contraction shortens** the muscle. An **eccentric contraction lengthens** it. These are both **isotonic** contractions as they create movement. An **isometric** contraction occurs to hold a static position and does not create movement. The muscles will not change length as the muscle force is equal to the resistance.

Upward pull-up
Isotonic concentric contraction

Hold at the top
Isometric contraction

Release slowly downwards
Isotonic eccentric contraction

THE LUNGS AND GAS EXCHANGE

The pathway of air

1. As you breathe, air is drawn in through the **nose or mouth** into the **trachea**.

2. It passes into the **bronchi**,

3. And branches into the smaller **bronchioles**,

4. Which fills the **lungs**,

5. Where oxygen is diffused into the blood via smaller air sacs called **alveoli**.

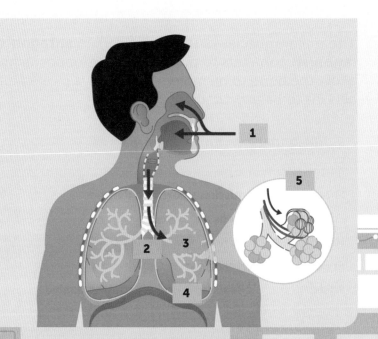

Gaseous exchange

The **alveoli** provide a very large surface area with **moist**, **thin** walls only **one cell thick**. This makes **diffusion** easier as the distance across one cell is so short. Lots of blood **capillaries** create a **strong blood supply** for the oxygen to diffuse into.

Two gases diffusing in opposite directions at the same time is called **gaseous exchange**. **Oxygen concentration** is lower in the capillaries than it is in the alveoli, so it passes through the capillary membrane into the blood as a result of diffusion. **Carbon dioxide** in the capillaries is in greater concentration than in the alveoli so it passes back through the other way into the lungs to be exhaled.

Oxygen combines with **haemoglobin** in the red blood cells to form **oxyhaemoglobin**. Haemoglobin can also carry carbon dioxide.

Gaseous exchange also takes place in the muscles where oxygen passes from the bloodstream to the muscles.

Explain how oxygen and carbon dioxide swap between the lungs and the bloodstream. [2]

The concentration of each gas will try equalise on both sides of the alveolo–capillary membrane.[1] so where there is greater concentration of one gas on one side, some will pass through to provide more oxygen in the blood or to remove excess carbon dioxide.[1]

BLOOD VESSELS

The body contains three different types of blood vessel: **arteries**, **veins** and **capillaries**.

The aorta branches into different arteries that carry blood to the major organs. These branch more and more until they form tiny vessels within tissues called capillaries which wrap around muscles and organs. Capillaries then join up to form veins.

Note that the muscle in arteries does **NOT** pump blood, it simply adjusts the size of the lumen.

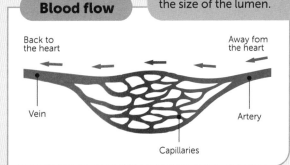

Blood flow

Back to the heart — Vein
Away from the heart — Artery
Capillaries

Blood vessel structure and function

	Arteries	Capillaries	Veins
	Thick outer wall, Small lumen, Thick layer of muscle and elastic fibre	Very small lumen, Very thin wall, only one cell thick	Thin layer of muscle and elastic fibres, Large lumen, Outer wall is fairly thin
Function	Carry **oxygenated** blood away from the heart	Exchange of substances with cells	Return **deoxygenated** blood at low pressure to the heart
Lumen	Narrow to maintain pressure	Very narrow. Keeps red blood cells close to tissue cells	Large, so there is less resistance to blood flow
Wall	Elastic fibres stretch and recoil to maintain pressure. Thick wall resists bursting	Very thin – Short distance to maximise **gas exchange** by diffusion	Low pressure so no need for a thick elastic wall
Valve	No – High pressure blood keeps moving	No	Yes – Prevents backflow of low pressure blood

Redistribution of blood

During exercise, the body redistributes blood to increase flow to the working muscles that most need the oxygen it carries. The body increases the width of the arteries, known as **vasodilation**, to increase flow to skeletal muscles. **Vasoconstriction** is the term given to the narrowing of blood vessels to restrict blood flow to tissues and organs that are not vital during maximal exercise.

The table below shows the distribution of blood at rest and during exercise. [2]

Destination	Rest	Maximal exercise
Skeletal muscles	19%	86%
Major organs	81%	

(a) Calculate the percentage of blood flow to the major organs during maximal exercise. [1]
(b) Give **one** reason for the redistribution of blood. [1]

(a) 14%.[1]

(b) To supply the skeletal muscles with the increased oxygen / nutrients they need during exercise.[1] To regulate temperature.[1]

STRUCTURE OF THE HEART.

The **heart** is an organ that pumps blood around the body.

The heart

The heart has walls made of cardiac muscle with **four chambers** inside. The **right ventricle** pumps deoxygenated blood to the lungs, where gas exchange takes place. The **left ventricle** pumps blood around the rest of the body. The **atria** collect blood as it returns and pump it into the ventricles. The atria contract together just before the ventricles contract. Blood shown as blue in the diagram has given up its oxygen to body cells – it is deoxygenated. The blood shown as red has been oxygenated in the lungs. **Valves** between the atria and ventricles, and in the veins, open due to pressure and close to prevent blood flowing backwards.

The **cardiac cycle** is as follows:

1. Atrial diastole (filling)
2. Ventricular diastole (filling)
3. Atrial systole (contraction)
4. Ventricular systole (contraction)

Double circulatory system.

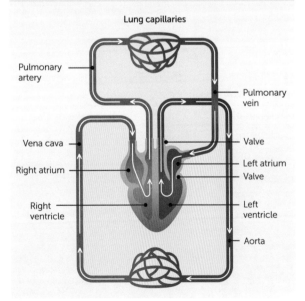

Complete the figure to show the pathway of the blood around the heart. [5]

Starting at the right ventricle, reorder statements 2–6 to show the pathway of the blood:

1. *Deoxygenated blood fills the right atrium (in the diastole process)* — `1`
   ↓
2. Then into the left ventricle — ▢
   ↓
3. Gas exchange occurs (blood is oxygenated) — ▢
   ↓
4. It then flows into the right ventricle — ▢
   ↓
5. Pulmonary vein transports oxygenated blood back to the left atrium — ▢
   ↓
6. The pulmonary artery then transports deoxygenated blood to the lungs — ▢
   ↓
7. *Before oxygenated blood is ejected and transported to the body via the aorta.* — `7`

One mark for each statement in the correct order: 1, 4,[1] 6,[1] 3,[1] 5,[1] 2,[1] 7.

When your blood pressure is monitored, a reading of 120/80 is considered healthy. 120 means the **systolic pressure** when the chambers eject blood to empty them. 80 is the **diastolic pressure** when the chambers relax to refill.

CARDIAC OUTPUT, STROKE VOLUME AND HEART RATE

Heart rate and stroke volume

Heart rate is the frequency with which the heart contracts (beats). It is measured in **beats per minute**. The natural resting heart rate is controlled by a group of cells found in the right atrium. They act as a **pacemaker**, producing regular impulses that travel through the heart causing it to contract.

Heart rate naturally increases during exercise to supply the muscles with the additional oxygen they need. Before exercise, **adrenaline** will cause the heart to rise in **anticipation**.

Stroke volume is the volume of blood pumped out of the heart by each ventricle during one contraction.

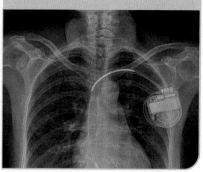

Artificial pacemakers are electrical devices used to correct irregularities in the heart rate.

Cardiac output

The volume of blood ejected from the heart in one minute is called the **cardiac output**. It is calculated from the stroke volume and the heart rate.

Cardiac output (Q) = stroke volume (mL) × heart rate (beats per minute)

1. A person has a resting stroke volume of 60 mL/beat and a heart rate of 65 beats per minute (bpm). Calculate the cardiac output. [2]
2. The following heart rate graph shows the data from a cyclist's training session.
   (a) Explain why the heart rate increased before exercise began at 8 mins. [2]
   (b) Suggest what might have caused a changed in heart rate at 13 mins and 17 mins. [1]

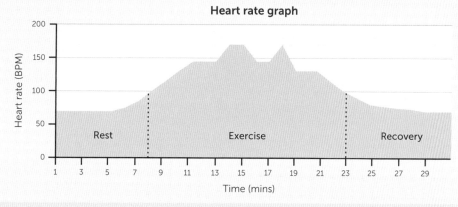

Heart rate graph

1. 60 × 65 = 3900[1] mL per minute / 3.9 litres per minute.[1]
2. (a) Before exercise, adrenaline[1] will cause an anticipatory[1] rise in heart rate.
   (b) A hill / greater resistance[1] could create a more intense period of exertion.

MECHANICS OF BREATHING

Changes in air pressure cause inhalation and exhalation. The rate of inhalation and exhalation can be controlled through the use of chest and abdominal muscles.

Inhaling and exhaling

The **rib cage**, **intercostal muscles** (those between the ribs) and the **diaphragm** control breathing. When inhaling, negative air pressure is created within the lungs to draw in a breath of air. Air always moves from areas of high pressure to areas of low pressure to create an equilibrium of pressure. In the process of taking in a breath:

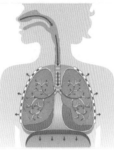

Inhalation

1. The diaphragm contracts, moving downwards from a dome shape to a flatter shape.
2. The intercostal muscles contract moving the rib cage up and out.
3. This increases the volume inside the chest cavity;
4. Which decreases the pressure inside the chest cavity.
5. A pressure gradient is created, pulling air into the lungs through the nose or mouth.

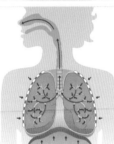

Exhalation

1. The diaphragm relaxes and returns to a dome shape.
2. The intercostal muscles relax moving the rib cage down and back.
3. This decreases the volume inside the chest cavity;
4. Which increases the pressure inside the chest cavity.
5. A pressure gradient is created and air is pushed out.

The effect of exercise on breathing

During exercise, inhalation and exhalation need to happen more quickly to allow the lungs to diffuse more oxygen into the bloodstream. The lungs can also expand more on **inspiration** (breathing in) with the use of the **pectoral muscles** and **sternocleidomastoid**. During **expiration** (breathing out), the rib cage is pulled down to force air out more quickly with use of the **abdominal muscles**.

Complete the table by adding **one** tick to each row to show how each of the following skeletal muscles help in the breathing process during exercise. [3]

Muscle	Helps with inhalation?	Helps with exhalation?
Abdominals		
Pectoral muscles		
Sternocleidomastoid		

Inhalation: pectoral[1] muscles and sternocleidomastoid.[1] Exhalation: abdominals.[1]

INTERPRETATION OF A SPIROMETER TRACE

A **spirometer** is a device used to measure lung volumes, such as the amount of air inhaled and exhaled in each breath. A device reading is called a **trace**.

A spirometer trace at rest and during exercise

Tidal volume

Tidal volume is the volume of air inhaled or exhaled per breath. At rest, tidal volume is approximately 500ml.

Residual volume

Residual volume is the amount of air left in the lungs even after trying to exhale as much as possible. The air left prevents the walls of the bronchioles and alveoli from sticking together. Residual volume does not change, even during exercise.

Inspiratory and expiratory reserve volumes

Inspiratory reserve volume and **expiratory reserve volume** indicate the amount of air that can forcefully be inhaled or exhaled. This is the additional volume of air that isn't normally used in regular breathing. During exercise, the inspiratory and expiratory reserve volumes both reduce, as tidal volume increases.

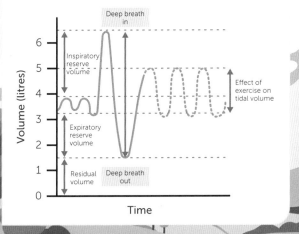

Exercise can change the volumes on a spirometer trace.

(a) State what is meant by 'tidal volume'. [1]

(b) Describe the effect of exercise on the readings from the spirometer trace. Refer to the tidal volume, expiratory reserve volume, the inspiratory reserve volume and the residual volume in your answer. [4]

(a) *The volume of air inspired or expired per breath.*[1]

(b) *The tidal volume will increase,*[1] *reducing*[1] *the inspiratory and expiratory reserve volumes.*[1] *The residual volume will not change.*[1]

AEROBIC AND ANAEROBIC EXERCISE

Aerobic exercise means being in the presence of, or using oxygen.
Anaerobic exercise occurs when the heart and lungs cannot supply blood and oxygen to muscles as fast as the respiring cells need them.

Aerobic exercise

During **aerobic exercise**, like marathon running, the relatively low intensity of the activity allows for the heart and lungs to provide enough oxygen for the muscles to use as they work. As a result, the activity can be sustained for a long period of time (duration). Examples include:

> Marathon running

> 2000m rowing

> Distance cycling

> Gentle skipping

Oxygen mixes with the glucose in the body to produce energy to fuel muscle movement. Waste products are water (sweat) and carbon dioxide (through increased exhalation).

Summary of aerobic exercise:

(glucose + oxygen →
energy + carbon dioxide + water)

Anaerobic exercise

During **anaerobic** exercise, like sprinting, the high intensity of the activity doesn't allow the heart and lungs to provide enough oxygen for the muscles to use as they work. The activity is too intense for delivery to keep up with demand. As a result, muscles are forced to work without enough oxygen, and **lactic acid** is produced as a waste product. The lactic acid causes pain and fatigue so these activities can only be sustained for a short period of time (duration). Examples include:

> Sprinting

> Heavy weightlifting

> Cycling sprints

> Long jump

Summary of anaerobic exercise:

(glucose → energy + lactic acid)

> The duration and/or intensity of a physical activity generally determine if it is aerobic or anaerobic.

Discuss whether swimming should be considered aerobic or anaerobic. [5]

A 10k swim would be performed over a long period of time[1] with moderate exertion throughout and little or no opportunity to rest[1] which is aerobic.[1] Sufficient oxygen would be available for energy to be produced to maintain muscle contractions.[1]

A competitive 50m race would be of high intensity and could not be sustained for long.[1] Lactic acid would be produced by the muscles owing to a lack of oxygen[1] which is anaerobic[1] as the blood uses its own blood sugar and/or glycogen stores as an alternative energy source given the lack of oxygen.[1]

Depending on the intensity of the swimming, and the period of time over which it is done, it could be considered as either.[1]

EXCESS POST-EXERCISE OXYGEN CONSUMPTION AND THE RECOVERY PROCESS

Excess post-exercise oxygen consumption or **EPOC** refers to continued heavy breathing or increased tidal volume once exercise has finished. This is also known as **oxygen debt**.

EPOC or oxygen debt

During vigorous exercise, the muscles respire anaerobically, producing lactic acid as a result of having insufficient oxygen. After exercise, a debt of oxygen has built up which needs to be repaid by maintaining a high breathing rate. The elevated level of oxygen helps to remove lactic acid by converting it back into glucose, and subsequently into carbon dioxide and water.

The recovery process from vigorous exercise

Cool down

Cooling down after exercise with a few minutes of **light physical activity** helps to maintain an **elevated breathing rate** and **heart rate** (blood flow). This eases the body out of exercise and provides continued blood flow and increased oxygen to the active muscles, which helps with the **removal of lactic acid**.

As a result of dynamic work, muscles will have contracted and increased in tension. **Stretching** encourages them to return to their resting length and reduces stiffness and soreness.

Manipulation of diet

Drinking water to **rehydrate** is essential to replace the fluids lost through perspiration (**sweat**) and water vapour on the breath. After exercise, eating **carbohydrates** helps to restore **glucose** levels (stored in the body as **glycogen**), especially if consumed in the first 24 hours after exercise. This is particularly important after endurance activities where large amounts of glycogen will have been used through the activity. Foods high in carbohydrate include pasta, rice and bread.

Ice baths or massage

Delayed Onset Muscle Soreness (**DOMS**) is the term given for the ache felt in muscles a day or two after an intense activity as they repair themselves. An **ice bath** immediately after exercise helps to reduce swelling caused by tiny tears and increases blood flow to the muscles – both of which help to reduce DOMS. **Massage** also reduces the effect of DOMS by increasing blood flow.

Describe how a footballer could aide their recovery after an intense match. [4]

Answer may include: Cool down with light exercise[1] to slowly lower the heart rate to normal.[1] Drink plenty of water to rehydrate,[1] replacing water[1] and minerals lost through sweat.
Take an ice bath[1] to reduce DOMS.[1] Gently stretch[1] while the muscles are still warm.[1] Eat simple carbohydrates[1] to replenish glycogen stores.[1]

THE SHORT- AND LONG-TERM EFFECTS OF EXERCISE

The effects of exercise depend on the period over which activity is undertaken.

Immediate effects of exercise (During exercise)

Hot, **sweaty**, **red skin** is caused by an increase in temperature as a result of lost energy, sweat glands trying to cool the skin, and the dilation of blood vessels below the skin to reduce body temperature.

An increase in depth and frequency of breathing happens to bring more air (and therefore oxygen) into the lungs so that the heart and blood vessels can deliver it to the working muscles faster. Increased exhalation also removes carbon dioxide more quickly.

Heart rate increases to pump newly oxygenated blood to the working muscles and to remove waste carbon dioxide.

Short-term effects of exercise (Up to 36 hours after exercise)

Tiredness or **fatigue** sets in as energy supplies decrease.

Aching muscles are caused by a failure to cool down or stretch properly while the muscles are still warm.

Delayed Onset of **Muscle Soreness** (**DOMS**) is caused by micro tears in the muscles as a result of heavy use.

Light-headedness can occur as a result of dehydration, low oxygen and low energy (glucose) stores. Overexertion can also cause a drop in blood pressure which can cause light-headedness.

Nausea (feeling sick) can occur as a result of reduced blood flow to the stomach and intestines. This is especially likely if a person has eaten too close to exercise.

Cramp is caused by a lack of glucose or electrolytes (salts and minerals) lost through sweat that can be replaced through foods and rehydration.

Long-term effects of exercise (Months and years of exercising)

The long-term effects of exercise can make significant, gradual improvements in specific **components of fitness** (see **pages 30 - 35** listing and measuring the components). The exact benefits of exercise depend on the type of activities that are undertaken.

Body shape may change, for example, by lowering body fat and increasing muscle mass which can help with strength and speed. This may also help with agility and flexibility.

Improved stamina, which helps you perform for longer.

Lower resting heart rate (bradycardia) as a healthier, more muscular, heart can achieve a higher stroke volume, delivering sufficient oxygen to a resting body with greater efficiency and therefore in fewer beats.

Greater muscle strength and **improved muscular endurance** which can increase power and explosive strength in a rugby game for example.

Improved speed, **suppleness** and **cardiovascular endurance** can all be achieved depending on the specific exercises undertaken. This can help with agility, flexibility and aerobic power.

Increased size of the heart (**cardiac hypertrophy**) which means it can pump more blood around the body per minute, increasing oxygen to the muscles and carrying more waste products away.

Hypertrophy is the name given to the enlargement of muscles through micro-tears that heal, increasing mass.

Explain why cardiac hypertrophy can result in bradycardia. [3]

Cardiac hypertrophy is an increase in the size of the heart[1] which means that stroke volume can increase / more blood is ejected per beat.[1] Increasing the size of the heart[1] means that it can pump an increased volume of blood around the body with each cycle.[1] As the body size remains the same, the heart no longer needs to work as hard to deliver sufficient blood to the organs at rest[1] so the heart rate lowers.[1]

EXAMINATION PRACTICE 1

01 Which **one** of the following bones is located at the hip? [1]

☐ A – Femur

☐ B – Scapula

☐ C – Talus

☐ D – Tibia

02 Which **one** of these statements defines abduction at the shoulder? [1]

☐ A – A rotational movement of the humerus

☐ B – An isometric contraction of the deltoid

☐ C – Raising the arms above the head

☐ D – The movement of an arm away from the midline of the body

03 Which **one** of the following describes the correct pathway of the blood as it leaves the heart via the aorta? [1]

☐ A – Left atrium → left ventricle → right atrium → right ventricle

☐ B – Right atrium → right ventricle → left atrium → left ventricle

☐ C – Right ventricle → left ventricle → right atrium → left atrium

☐ D – Right ventricle → right atrium → left ventricle → left atrium

04 Which **one** of the following is an immediate effect of exercise? [1]

☐ A – Improved muscular endurance

☐ B – Improved speed

☐ C – Increased heart rate

☐ D – Increased size of the heart

05 Give **three** functions of the skeleton. [3]

06 Tendons, ligaments and bursae are both found at major synovial joints.

06.1 Explain **two** differences between tendons and ligaments. [2]

06.2 State the function of bursae in the prevention of injury. [1]

07 Lee lifts himself into the upwards plank position in Position B.

| Position A | Position B |

07.1 Identify the muscular contraction and the associated muscle at the elbow as Lee lifts himself into Position B. [2]

07.2 Explain why holding a high plank in position B is an example of isometric contraction. [2]

07.3 Give **one** other sporting example of an isometric contraction. [1]

08   Petra takes a free throw in basketball.

08.1 Explain how Petra's skeleton and muscular system work together to produce the
      movement required for the free throw.   [3]

A spirometer trace for Petra before the game is shown below.

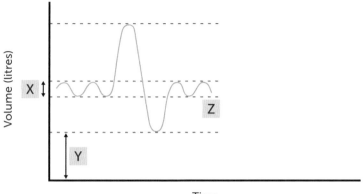

Time

08.2 Label the lung volumes marked X and Y on the trace.   [2]

08.3 Draw an extension of the trace at point Z to show the likely effect of exercise during the
      game on Petra's breathing.   [2]

08.4 During a particularly intense period of gameplay, Petra's heart rate was recorded at 170 beats
      per minute.

      Her stroke volume was 70 ml.

      Calculate Petra's cardiac output in litres.   [2]

08.5 Name **one** additional muscle that helps Petra's diaphragm and intercostal muscles to take
      a deeper breath when she needs it during intense exercise.   [1]

08.6 One cardiac cycle is completed when each of the diastole and systole phases have
      been completed.

      Define what is meant by diastole and systole.   [2]

09.   Discuss how long-term fitness training may improve an ice skater's performances.   [6]

10.   An EPOC graph is shown below. Label area X.   [1]

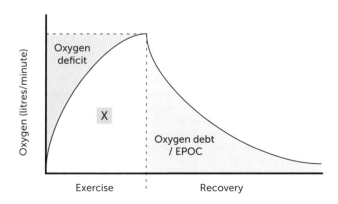

LEVER SYSTEMS

There are three classes of lever system in the body. Each lever system has a fulcrum, load and effort.

Fulcrums, load and effort

Levers involve a rigid bar (bone) that pivots or rotates about a fulcrum (joint) with a load applied. A lever system comprises:

A **fulcrum** or pivot around which a force is exerted. (In the body, this is a joint.)

A **load** (or **resistance**) being moved. (In the body this relates to bodyweight and any additional load being carried.)

The **effort** or force required to move the load. (Muscular effort.)

First, second and third class lever systems

First class lever

First class levers have the fulcrum between the effort and the load or resistance, like a see-saw.

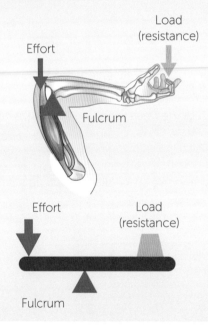

Effort

Load (resistance)

Fulcrum

Effort

Load (resistance)

Fulcrum

An Internazionale player throws the ball in during a UEFA Champions League match.

1. Identify the type of lever system working at the knee in the upward phase of a squat. [1]
2. Identify the lever system that is used to go up onto the toes when pushing off the blocks in a sprint start. [1]

1. *Third class lever.*[1]
2. *Second class lever.*[1]

FLE 123 is a useful mnemonic to remember the lever classes.
A class 1 has the *Fulcrum* in the middle.
A class 2 has the *Load* in the middle
A class 3 has the *Effort* in the middle.

Second class lever

Second class levers are most easily remembered as having a wheelbarrow action. The fulcrum is at one end with the effort at the opposite end. The load or resistance is anywhere in the middle.

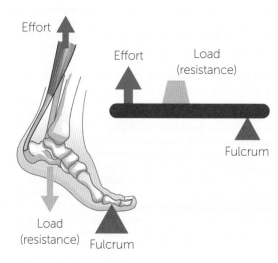

An athlete takes advantage of a class 2 lever action with plantar flexion at the ankle to leave the take off board with explosive power at a long jump event.

Think about where the muscle attaches to the bone when considering what type of lever system applies to an action.

Third class lever

A class 3 lever has the fulcrum at one end, the load at the opposite end and the effort applied in the middle.

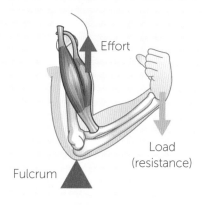

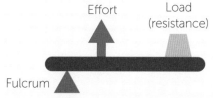

An athlete uses his biceps to flex at the elbow in a class 3 lever action to draw the paddle through the water in the Men's Kayak Sprint 200m at the Olympic Games in Rio.

MECHANICAL ADVANTAGE

A lever is a very simple way to gain mechanical advantage (MA), making lifting or moving much easier.

Calculating mechanical advantage

A lever has a mechanical advantage if its effort arm is longer than its load arm. By comparing the distance of the effort and the load from the fulcrum, you can determine the degree of mechanical advantage. A lever with mechanical advantage is a more efficient lever and will be able to move heavier loads with relatively little effort.

Mechanical advantage = effort arm ÷ weight (resistance/load) arm

A **first class lever** must have the effort further from the fulcrum than the load for it to have a mechanical advantage. The further away it is, the greater the advantage.

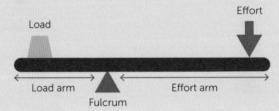

A **second class lever** always has a mechanical advantage of greater than 1 as the effort is always further from the fulcrum than the resistance. This means a heavy load can be lifted more efficiently.

A **third class lever** is said to have a **mechanical disadvantage** as the effort is always closer to the fulcrum than the resistance, or the effort arm is shorter than the resistance arm. Despite a mechanical disadvantage when it comes to load, class 3 levers increase distance, so a short muscle movement produces a greater output movement. The hip joint is an example of a class 3 lever, producing large movements of the femur with relatively small movement near the fulcrum (ball joint).

A tennis player makes a backhand volley.

(a) Identify the type of lever acting in the extension of the elbow during the stroke. [1]

(b) Explain the mechanical advantage or disadvantage of this lever system. [3]

(a) First class lever.[1]

(b) A mechanical disadvantage occurs[1] as the effort (tricep muscle) is closer to the fulcrum[1] (elbow) than the load[1] (tennis racket in the hand at the end of the forearm). However, a short tricep movement creates a large forearm movement to hit the ball with force.[1]

ANALYSIS OF BASIC UPPER-BODY MOVEMENTS IN SPORTING EXAMPLES

Elbow action in push-ups and football throw ins

Flexion and extension change the angle at a joint.

Flexion at the elbows in the downward phase of a push up.

Flexion at the elbows in a football throw in.

Extension at the elbows during the upward phase of the movement.

Extension at the elbows as the ball is released.

Shoulder action in a cricket bowl

The arm circumducts and rotates within the ball and socket joint at the shoulder during a cricket bowl.

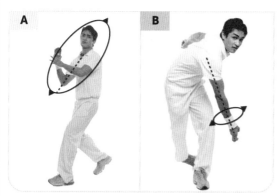

A   Circumduction of the arm around the shoulder during a cricket bowl.

B   Rotation of the arm along its axis in the shoulder joint during a cricket bowl.

ANALYSIS OF BASIC LOWER-BODY MOVEMENTS IN SPORTING EXAMPLES

Hip, knee and ankle action in running

Hip flexion

Ankle plantarflexion

Knee extension

Ankle dorsiflexion

Hip extension

Knee flexion

A full sprint stride in three stages

Hip, knee and ankle action in kicking

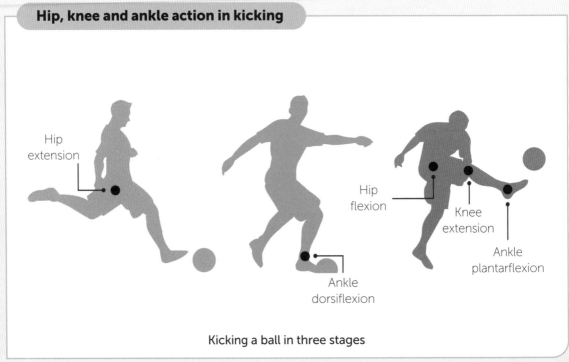

Hip extension

Hip flexion

Knee extension

Ankle plantarflexion

Ankle dorsiflexion

Kicking a ball in three stages

Hip, knee and ankle action in a standing vertical jump

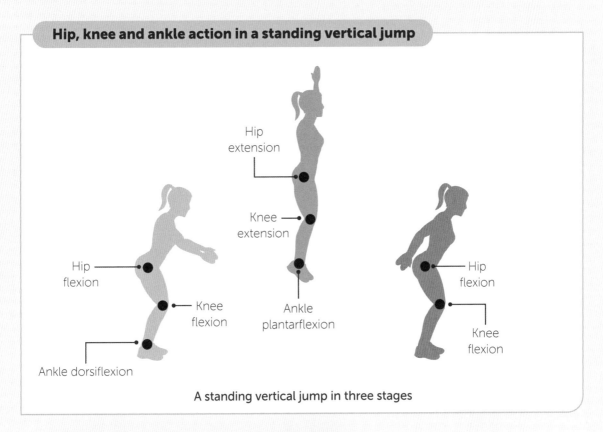

A standing vertical jump in three stages

Hip, knee and ankle action in basic squats

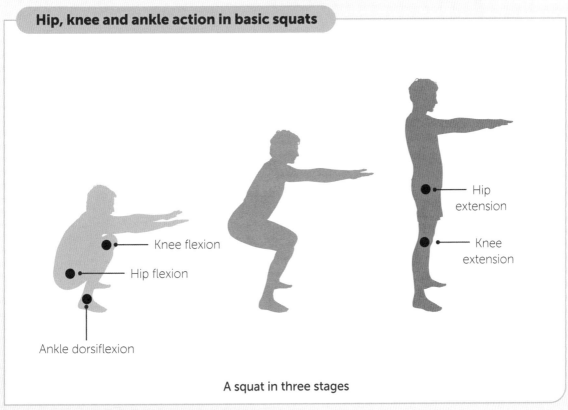

A squat in three stages

PLANES AND AXES OF MOVEMENT

There are three planes and three axes of movement used whilst performing sporting actions.

Planes and axes

A **plane** of movement is an imaginary flat surface across which the body moves in an action. An **axis** of movement is an imaginary line through the body, about which the body rotates.

Movements occur *in* a plane and *around* an axis, so the plane and the axis for a movement should be revised together as pairs.

Sagittal & transverse	Frontal & sagittal	Transverse & longitudinal
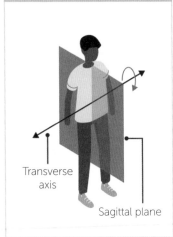		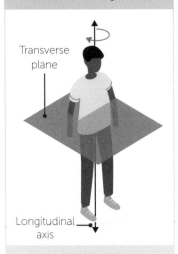
Typical movements	**Typical movements**	**Typical movements**
Running, flexion and extension actions take place in the **sagittal** plane.	Sidestepping and sideways adduction and abduction use the **frontal plane**.	Twisting, rotating or spinning actions happen in the **transverse plane**.
Bending and rolling actions take place around the **transverse axis**.	Cartwheels take place around the **sagittal axis**.	Spinning (e.g. ice skating) and pivoting happen around the **longitudinal axis**.

Figure 1 shows a discus thrower. Identify the plane and axis of movement used in throwing the discus. [2]

Transverse plane.[1]
Longitudinal axis.[1]

Figure 1

An example sporting action using the sagittal plane and the transverse axis

A forward roll or somersault involves moving in the sagittal plane, bending and rotating at the waist around the transverse axis.

An example sporting action using the frontal plane and the sagittal axis

A cartwheel involves moving sideways in the frontal plane, whilst rotating the body sideways around the navel around the sagittal axis.

EXAMINATION PRACTICE 2

01   A field athlete is shown below, preparing to throw a javelin.

01.1   Identify the class of lever acting at the elbow as the arm extends at the elbow to throw
       the javelin.   [1]

01.2   Draw a fully labelled diagram to show the class of lever identified in question 01.1.   [2]

Figure A	Figure B

02   Figures A and B show diagrams of an ice skater moving across the ice and into a spin.

02.1   Identify the plane and axis of movement used in raising the leg from figure A to figure B.   [2]

02.2   Identify the plane and axis of movement used in performing a spin on the ice in figure B.   [2]

02.3   The skater jumps into a spin using a third-class lever at the hip and knee.

       Identify the joint movement at the hip and knee of the driving leg on take off in a jump.   [1]

02.4   Explain why a class three lever has no mechanical advantage.   [2]

02.5   To maintain balance in figure A, the skater uses abduction.

       Define abduction using an example from Figure A.   [1]

HEALTH AND FITNESS

Health and fitness are related but they are not the same thing.
Exercise plays a role in both.

Health

Health is defined as a **person's complete state of physical, mental and social well-being and not merely the absence of disease or infirmity**. All physiological systems need to be in positive, balanced harmony. Decreased health may affect the intensity, regularity and desire to train or exercise, lowering fitness.

Fitness

Fitness describes **a person's ability to effectively meet or cope with the demands of their physical environment**. They should be able to physically perform an activity or task without increased risk of injury. Fitness can still be increased despite poor health, for example if someone has an unhealthy diet, but is still able to train.

Mohammed said that "Abdi is healthy because he is not physically ill or frail".

(a) Explain what is incorrect about this statement. [2]

(b) Give **two** ways that health may be improved through greater fitness. [2]

(a) *Abdi could have low self esteem / stress / depression / suffer from loneliness / poor posture / high blood pressure / alcohol or drug abuse / smoking habit / poor diet[1] which may not impact his physical condition / impacts his complete state of well-being.[1]*

(b) *Answers may include two from: Reduced chance of illness and disease / better sleep patterns / improved posture and personal image / stronger heart and reduced risk of heart disease / lower blood pressure / reduced risk of diabetes through reduced body fat / better social life if training together with others.*

THE COMPONENTS OF FITNESS

Each of the components of fitness can be linked to various sports. They can help to plan, carry out, monitor and evaluate exercise and training programmes to suit individual needs.

Agility – The ability to move and change direction quickly (at speed) whilst maintaining control.

Rugby players need agility to side step around opposing defence players to avoid a tackle and gain territory.

Balance – The maintenance of the centre of mass over the base of support. Balance may be static (still) or dynamic (whilst moving).

Windsurfers and **horse riders** need excellent balance to continually adjust their centre of mass to stay on top of their boards and horses as they move.

Cardiovascular endurance (aerobic power) – The ability of the heart and lungs to supply oxygen to the working muscles.

Marathon and endurance runners need to be able to maintain a high volume of oxygenated blood to the working muscles for a long period.

Coordination – The ability to use two or more body parts together smoothly and efficiently.

Ball and racket sports require excellent hand, eye and body coordination in order to strike the ball cleanly on a consistent basis.

Flexibility – The range of movements possible at a joint.

Gymnasts, divers, martial artists and **figure skaters** require excellent flexibility to increase their range of movement and to reduce injury.

Reaction time – The time taken to initiate a response to a stimulus.

Muscular endurance – The ability of a muscle or muscle group to undergo repeated contractions, without fatigue.

Triathletes require muscular endurance for running, swimming and cycling to reduce fatigue in muscles repeatedly contracting.

Sprint racers need to react to a starting gun quickly. **Boxers** need to avoid punches.

Strength – The ability to overcome a resistance (maximal, static, dynamic and explosive): **Maximal strength** is the absolute maximum force that can be generated in one muscle contraction. **Static strength** is the ability to hold a body part or limb in a still position. **Dynamic strength** is the ability to apply force when the muscles are continually contracting and extending. **Explosive strength** (**power**) is the product of strength and speed, i.e. strength × speed.

Speed – The ability to move body parts to perform an action quickly.

High maximal strength is required in **boxing** and **weightlifting**.

Static strength helps **rugby** players to hold the resistance in a scrum position.

Gymnasts have high dynamic strength.

Explosive strength (power), is crucial in **sprint sports**, **boxing**, **shot put** and **volleyball** to provide bursts of power when needed. For example, to get out of the blocks first, create a final burst to the finish line, put a shot or smash a ball with strength and speed.

Sprinters and **tennis players** require speed to move quickly across the track or court.

The reasons for and limitations of fitness testing

The components of fitness can be tested, but these tests do not always provide helpful results.

The reasons for fitness testing

- To identify strengths and/or weaknesses in a performance or the success of a training programme
- To monitor improvement
- To show a starting level of fitness
- To inform training requirements
- To compare against norms of the group, and national averages
- To motivate and set goals
- To provide variety in a training programme

The limitations of fitness testing

- Tests are often not sport specific or too general
- They may not replicate the movements of activity
- They do not replicate the competitive conditions required in sports
- Many tests do not use direct measuring or they do not push subjects to their maximum likely to be experienced in real conditions as it could be dangerous in regular testing – therefore results can be inaccurate and some have questionable reliability
- Tests must be carried out with the correct procedures to increase validity

Explain how a rock climber would require high static and dynamic strength. [2]

Static strength is required in hand holds / grip strength when holding their weight / foot holds when standing on a ledge.[1] Dynamic strength is necessary to repeatedly lift their own weight when moving up the rock face / leaping and securing a hold.[1]

MEASURING THE COMPONENTS OF FITNESS

There are various specific tests that can be used to measure different aspects of fitness. Each one is carried out and organised differently.

Illinois Agility Test Agility

This test measures agility. It requires **eight cones**, carefully arranged at measured distances apart as shown in the diagram. The performer starts face down and runs against a **stopwatch timer** to the end. The activity is measured in seconds.

Try out each test where you have the right equipment and measure your performance against national standards and average scores available online.

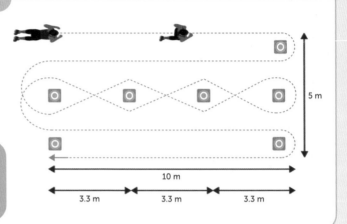

Stork Stand Test Balance

The Stork Stand Test requires a **stopwatch** and an **assistant**.

Time is recorded in seconds.

See **page 37** for national ratings.

1 Start from a balanced position on two feet.

2 Place hands on hips.

3 Place one foot on the inside of the knee of the standing leg.

4 Lift the heel of the standing leg when stopwatch is started.

5 Stop the timer when balance is lost or when the foot moves from the inside leg.

Evaluate the appropriateness of the Stork Stand Test for a gymnast and a cyclist. [6]

The stork stand test is a maximal test of static balance.[✓] A gymnast needs excellent static balance which this measures.[✓] Gymnasts often need to balance on one leg which is also measured in this test[✓] A cyclist requires good balance but not on their own feet[✓] and would not replicate the movements of their sport so closely[✓] so the test results may not be such a reliable measure of performance.[✓] The test could be useful to measure improvement in balance for both athletes.[✓] Overall, the test would be better for identifying strengths and weaknesses in a gymnast's balance than a cyclist's.[✓] This question should be marked in according with the levels-based mark scheme on page 117.

Multi Stage Fitness Test Cardiovascular endurance / aerobic power

Cones, an **assistant** and a **measuring tape** of at least 20m in length are required to set up the test. An **audio player** and **recording of the bleeps** is also required at the start.

When the assistant begins playing the recording of the bleeps, the participant must run 20 metres to reach the other cone before the next bleep. The time interval between bleeps gets progressively shorter, requiring faster and faster shuttle runs between the cones. Failure to reach the cone before the bleep twice in a row ends the test, and the last properly completed level should be recorded. The score is usually recorded as a level and bleep number, for example 5/7. (Level 5, bleep 7.)

Bleep!   Bleep!

20 metres

Wall Toss Test Coordination

The **Wall Toss Test** measures **hand-eye coordination**. It requires a **tennis ball**, a **flat wall**, some **marker tape** or **chalk**, and a **stopwatch**.

1. Mark a point or line 2 metres away from a flat wall.
2. Stand at the line with both feet together facing the wall.
3. Start the stopwatch or timer for 30 seconds.
4. Throw the ball at the wall with one hand and catch it in the other.
5. Repeat this, throwing from one hand to the other as many times as possible in the time.
6. Record the score counting each successful catch as 1.

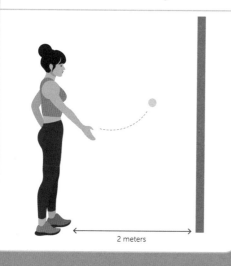

2 meters

Sit and Reach Test Flexibility

Using a **sit and reach box**, the athlete sits on the floor with their bare feet flat against the box and their legs straight. The athlete then reaches forwards as far as possible to move the slider. The slider records how far in centimetres they are from zero (their feet).

Sit-Up Bleep Test Muscular endurance

The **sit-up bleep test** requires a partner to support the feet and ankles, and to press play on an audio recording of progressively faster bleeps. The participant sits up and back down again to the rhythm of the bleeps. As a **maximal test**, the sit ups continue until the participant can no longer keep time with the bleeps. The score is equal to the number of sit ups performed.

Discuss the suitability of the vertical jump test for measuring the explosive power of a javelin thrower. [5]

The vertical jump test largely measures the power of the legs, whereas a javelin thrower's power needs to come predominately from the arm and shoulder.[1] A javelin thrower needs a more muscular body, adding bodyweight which would be harder to lift in a vertical jump.[1] Jumping does not replicate the movements of javelin throwing so would not be so useful as a performance measure.[1] As a maximal test, it can help to motivate and push performance.[1] Legs are involved in javelin throwing, so measuring their power is helpful.[1]

Vertical Jump Test Power or explosive strength / Anaerobic power

The **vertical jump test** involves a **wall**, a **ruler** or **measuring tape**, and some **chalk** to make a mark with. With flat feet, stand and reach up the wall as high as possible and record the height.

Now, jump as high as possible using your arms and legs and make a mark using chalked hands or ask an assistant to record the height. Measure the distance between the standing reach height and the jump height in centimetres.

Ruler Drop Test Reaction time

Requirements: A **metre rule** and an **assistant**.

1. The assistant holds the metre rule vertically at the zero end.

2. The participant places their thumb and forefingers around the stick at the 50 cm mark but without touching it.

3. The stick is released by the assistant without warning.

4. The participant must close their fingers around the stick as fast as possible to catch it.

5. The score is the distance in centimetres from the catching point to the original 50cm mark.

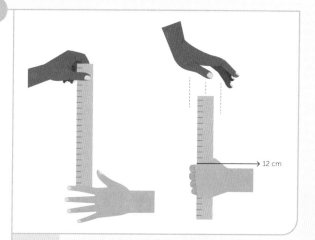

12 cm

One Rep Max Test Maximal strength

This **one rep max** (**1RM**) test commonly uses a **bar bell**, **bench** or **leg press machine**. It is used to determine the maximum weight that a particular muscle group can lift in one **repetition** (rep).

Choose an appropriate piece of weight lifting equipment for the muscle group being tested.

1. Lift an appropriate starting weight once. Use a spotter if necessary.
2. Increase the weight and lift again.
3. Repeat until the participant can no longer lift one rep.
4. Record the weight (usually in kg) of the last successful lift.

30 Metre Sprint Test Speed

The 30 metre sprint test measures speed. Describe how to carry out this test. [3]

Use 2 cones[1] and place them 30 metres apart[1] using a tape measure.[1] Allow a flying start to the sprint[1] and with a stop watch, time the athlete running as they pass between the start and end cones.[1] Record the time in seconds.[1]

Handgrip Dynamometer Test Strength

This measures **grip strength**. Using a handgrip dynamometer in the dominant hand, squeeze the handle with maximum effort keeping the elbow at 90 degrees. Record the best score.

DEMONSTRATION OF HOW DATA IS COLLECTED FOR FITNESS TESTING

The results of testing are often recorded as numeric values, comments and opinions. They can also be compared to national averages.

Measurements

Measurements are usually taken and recorded in **seconds**, **levels**, **centimetres** and **numbers**. Using numerical measurements, it becomes easy to compare one measurement with another. This may be a set of performances by a single athlete over time to look at progress, or those of a group of athletes to compare abilities.

Qualitative and quantitative data

Qualitative data

Qualitative data involves **subjective** information including opinions, feelings and emotions. It is usually verbal or written information and could be comparative, for example, *"I performed better than last time, but I could do better"*. See **page 52**.

Quantitative data

Quantitative data is **objective** information which can be defined without opinion. This is usually a numerical score, distance, time or level. An example would be *"Level 9/11 in the Multi stage fitness test"*. See **page 52**.

The standard national ratings for the Stork Stand Test are given below.

Rating	Males (seconds)	Females (seconds)
Excellent	> 50	> 30
Good	41–50	23–30
Average	31–40	16–22
Fair	20–30	10–15
Poor	< 20	< 10

Dina maintained the Stork Stand Test for 24, 26, 27, 29 and 28 seconds in her last five attempts. She said that she is "pleased with her progress but upset after the last test".

(a) Compared with the national standards, identify Dina's rating. [1]

(b) Using the **quantitative** information provided, describe her progress. [2]

(c) Using the **qualitative** information provided, describe her attitude to progression. [2]

(a) Good.[1]

(b) Generally improving[1] but may be plateauing / had an off-day.[1]

(c) She wants to improve and clearly cares[1] as she is upset/frustrated when she doesn't show progress.[1]

THE PRINCIPLES OF TRAINING AND OVERLOAD

The key principles of training and overload use mnemonics of SPORT and FITT.

Key principles of training

The key principles of training are provided as guidance when designing a training programme. Following the principles of training will help to make training effective.

SPORT includes:

S   Specificity

Training programmes developed to specifically link to your training goals, sport or energy systems. For example, to build specific muscle groups identified as needing improvement, or developing specific skills related to an athlete's sport such as free kicks, set pieces in field sports or finishing in track sports.

PO   Progressive Overload

As related terms, progress means to gradually increase the intensity of training so that fitness gains occur. Overload is required to push your body beyond its comfortable limits to provide challenge, overcome plateaus in development and drive progress.

R   Reversibility

Reversibility states that athletes will undo their progress if their training schedule lapses or becomes less demanding.

T   Tedium

Changing training schedules and activities to avoid boredom and repetition. Variety is needed.

Key principles of overload

The key principles of overload state that training should always overload the body's systems more than normal, by increasing the work it does to benefit from the long-term effects of exercise.

FITT includes:

F   Frequency

How often do training sessions happen? Two or three times a week is considered good but this may increase as required.

I   Intensity

How hard are the training sessions? Weights may be increased, resistance on a rowing machine may be increased or an incline may be introduced for runners.

T   Time

How long do sessions last for? As fitness increases, sessions, reps or sets may increase. Rest periods may also decrease.

T   Type

What type of training is done in each session? Switching between different types of training (see **pages 39–43**) adds variety, helps with overload, provides different fitness benefits and prevents tedium.

Samira is training for a basketball match. How can Samira use the training principles of **specificity** and **tedium** to improve her performance in the game? [2]

Specificity: Work on muscles / movement / energy systems used in basketball[1] / agility with a ball to replicate the movements in a game.[1] Increase standing jump performance by working on the legs.[1] Practice set pieces / drills.[1]
Tedium: Vary the training to avoid boredom.[1] Use agility training / leg workouts / interval training / static stretching to increase aerobic performance, agility and standing jump height.[1]

TYPES OF TRAINING

There are many different types of training, each with their own distinctions.

Circuit training

Circuit training involves roughly 6–12 **stations**, each with a different exercise designed to achieve the aims of the participants. Station activities will depend on the **space** and **equipment** available. The demand of a circuit can be altered according to the exercise or by changing the **work:rest ratio** to decrease rest and achieve overload more quickly.

Any training and practice method must take account of the purpose, the effects on the body and the recovery.

Advantages

- ⊕ Can be used by large groups.
- ⊕ Easy to set up.
- ⊕ Usually involves little equipment so it is inexpensive to organise.
- ⊕ Content or demand can be widely adapted to suit most training goals / components of fitness.
- ⊕ Can be tailored to train the whole body or specific parts of it.
- ⊕ Different intensities can be programmed to train aerobically and anaerobically.
- ⊕ Exercises can replicate specific sporting movements.

Disadvantages

- ⊖ Isolated exercises may not always be totally sport specific.
- ⊖ Does not replicate 'real time' match play situations or competition.
- ⊖ Technique can be affected by muscle fatigue which can increase the risk of injury.

1. State what is meant by the work:rest ratio. [1]

The period of time spent exercising at a station compared to rest periods in between stations or reps.

Continuous training

Continuous training involves sustained exercise at a **constant rate** (or **steady state**) with **no rest**. It involves **aerobic demand** for a minimum of 20 minutes, for example running, swimming, rowing or cycling.

Advantages

+ Improves cardiovascular and muscular endurance.
+ Increases muscular strength in active muscles.
+ Less intense on joints compared with other training methods.
+ Can change body shape over time to become an ectomorph / more streamlined.

Disadvantages

− Continuous nature may result in injury from repetitive contractions.
− May not increase power as it is not anaerobic.
− Can result in tedium / boredom.
− Longer training sessions can take a lot of time.

2. George is training for a marathon. He has chosen to use continuous training.

   Discuss whether continuous training is an effective training method for George. [5]

   Continuous training has a relatively low impact on joints and ligaments.[1] Continuous training by running can closely replicate the movements of a marathon[1] and requires no specialist equipment.[1] He is likely to improve his cardiovascular endurance and may improve his body shape,[1] reducing his weight[1] and increasing speed.[1] Continuous training is suitable for individuals as programmes need to be tailored which may suit George.[1]

   George may become bored[1] by running constantly so could vary exercise with cycling or swimming.[1] However, this would not replicate the movements of a marathon so closely.[1] George could supplement his training[1] with other techniques such as interval training and static stretching to increase strength and lengthen his stride / range of motion.[1]

Fartlek training

Fartlek is the Swedish term for 'speed play'. This involves **varying the speed**, **terrain** and **work:recovery ratios** of exercises. It is related to continuous training and interval training. Intensity is varied over different terrain, gradient or speed of activity.

Advantages

- Improves speed, cardiovascular and muscular endurance.
- Combines aerobic and anaerobic activity.
- Helps with pace and an awareness of your physical response to changes in intensity.

Disadvantages

- Needs to be tailored to the individual so unsuitable for groups.
- Requires discipline to continuously undertake unstructured exercise.
- Experience is required to ensure that training is at the right level of intensity.

3. Jo plays competitive rugby and is looking to improve her performance.

Evaluate the appropriateness of Fartlek training for Jo. [9]

AO1: Fartlek training is known as speed play. It generally involves running and changing the speed and terrain at different points in the run.[✓]

AO2/3: Fartlek training is ideal for game sports that consist of short bursts of anaerobic sprinting mixed with aerobic recovery periods.[✓] *(AO2) as it helps the body to cope with varying intensities of match play.*[✓] *(AO3) It helps to develop the use of power and explosive strength*[✓] *(AO2) which are needed during fast game play such as a sprint to the try line.*[✓] *(AO3) Lower intensity training improves cardiovascular endurance*[✓] *(AO2) which is necessary to get through a match without tiring at the end.*[✓] *(AO3) Mind/body awareness can also be improved*[✓] *(AO2) which helps Jo understand how her body may react to sudden changes in the demand she puts on it.*[✓] *(AO3) Jo may not be able to train using Fartlek with the whole team as the programme needs to be tailored to the individual which will differ according to their goals or player position.*[✓] *(AO3) This may reduce the opportunity for team bonding*[✓] *(AO3) and doesn't replicate true match conditions or gameplay.*[✓] *(AO3) Training may improve power*[✓] *(AO2) which will assist Jo with scrums, sprints and tackles.*[✓] *(AO3) Since Fartlek is often used during the playing season, injury during training may mean that she misses future fixtures.*[✓] *(AO3) Jo can use SPORT and FITT for safe and effective training.*[✓] *(AO2) Jo may combine her training with weight training, HIIT training or plyometrics*[✓] *(AO2) to improve all-round power and strength.*[✓] *(AO3)*

Tick marks are used for guidance on valid points. This question should be marked in accordance with the levels based mark scheme on page 117.

Interval training and high intensity interval training

Interval training involves periods of exercising hard, interspersed with periods of rest or low intensity exercise. **High intensity interval training** (**HIIT**) increases the level of demand and involves more active rest.

Advantages

- Develops aerobic and anaerobic fitness.
- Easily adapted for specific outcomes and fitness components.

Disadvantages

- Can be very tiring which requires discipline and motivation.
- Intensity can cause injury if not properly managed.

4. Matt is a hockey player.

Explain how interval training could be used to improve Matt's hockey performance. [2]

Training would use sprints / anaerobic bursts[1] interspersed with rests[1] which would mimic the demands / be specific to hockey[1] as performance is at different intensities.[1]
Hockey involves short bursts of high intensity movement / action[1] followed by active rest in slower parts of the game.[1]

Static stretching

A static stretch is one that is taken to the limit of your range of motion and held (isometrically) for up to 30 seconds. This increases flexibility. A correct technique is advisable to avoid over stretching.

Stretching is important for most sports as part of warm-ups and general flexibility.

Advantages

- Stretching increases flexibility and range of movement.
- Reduces injury in sport owing to greater flexibility.
- Safe enough for everyone to be able to do.

Disadvantages

- Some muscle groups are difficult to stretch.
- Poor technique, bouncing a stretch or over stretching can cause injury.
- Can take time to complete a full stretch of the whole body.

5. Justify why static stretching would be beneficial to the performance of **two** different sporting skills. [2]

Two from: A diver to maintain a neat tuck or pike position,[1] a hurdler raising the trailing leg over the hurdle,[1] a gymnast / figure skater for greater flexibility.[1] Answers are not exhaustive.

Weight training

Weight training involves lifting weights using different muscle groups to develop strength and muscular endurance. The choice of weight or exercise depends on the fitness aim. Weights may include free weights, medicine balls or resistance machines. A safe lifting technique, for example, using a straight back, is necessary to avoid injury. A spotter may also be required to ensure safety with free weights.

Advantages

- Exercises and reps are easily adapted for specific muscular strength or endurance.
- Can be done by anyone, using anything with resistance.

Disadvantages

- Poor technique and lifting too much can cause injury.
- Muscle ache a day or so after training / DOMS is common. See **page 15**.

6. Erik is a weight lifter.
   Explain how Erik can use weight training to improve maximal strength in his quadriceps. [2]

   Weights of almost the maximum weight that Erik can lift should be lifted a very low number of repetitions before resting.[1] He should repeat this for a few sets[1] with a short period of rest in between.[1]

Plyometric training

Plyometric training involves **hopping**, **bounding** or **jumping** to develop **power**, **speed** and **explosive strength**. Plyometrics make use of gravity to extend muscles (eccentric contraction) before making a larger concentric contraction. For example, jumping off a box into a deep squat to lengthen the quadriceps before jumping higher onto another box.

Advantages

- Simulates many sporting movements such as those in high jump, volleyball, sprint starts and javelin throwing.
- No specialist equipment required.

Disadvantages

- Requires a high level of fitness to start with, as there is a high risk of injury.
- Repetitive jumping and bounding can cause stress on the joints.

CALCULATING INTENSITIES TO OPTIMISE TRAINING EFFECTIVENESS

The **training threshold** is defined as the level of intensity required to produce an improvement in performance or adaptation of the body to better suit the sport.

Calculating the aerobic and anaerobic training zone

For training to be most effective, an athlete must remain in the correct training zone for their own fitness aims:

Maximum heart rate =	220 (Beats Per Minute) – Age
Aerobic training zone:	60% – 80% of maximal heart rate
Anaerobic training zone:	80% – 90% of maximal heart rate

Worked example

Abi is a 25 year old distance swimmer calculating her aerobic training zone:

$$220 - 25 = 195 \text{ BPM Maximum heart rate}$$
$$195 \times 0.8 = 156 \text{ BPM Upper training threshold at 80\% of MaxHR}$$
$$195 \times 0.6 = 117 \text{ BPM Lower training threshold at 60\% of MaxHR}$$

Abi should adapt her training so that her heart remains in the 117 – 156 BPM range in order to achieve maximum aerobic benefit.

1. The type of training should be adapted to ensure that the heart and body are working at the right level to achieve the fitness aims of the individual.

   (a) Give **two** ways in which circuit training can be altered to determine the fitness aim. [2]

   (b) Henry is a 30 year old lacrosse player. He is looking to increase the effectiveness of his circuit training by remaining in the anaerobic zone.

   Calculate the upper and lower threshold of his anaerobic training zone. [2]

   (a) Two from: Work / time exercising,[1] rest,[1] content.[1]

   (b) 220 – 30 = 190 BPM Maximum heart rate
   190 × 0.9 = 171[1] BPM Upper training threshold at 90% of MaxHR
   190 × 0.8 = 152[1] BPM Lower training threshold at 80% of MaxHR

Applying the one repetition maximum calculation

One repetition maximum (**one rep max**) is a calculation used in weight training to ensure that an athlete will receive maximum benefit from their training in accordance with their own fitness aims. It is calculated on **page 36** and used as follows:

Strength and power training	High weight with low reps	Maintain weights above 70% of one rep max	Complete approximately three sets of 4 to 8 reps
Muscular endurance	Low weight with high reps	Maintain weights below 70% of one rep max	Complete approximately three sets of 12 to 15 reps

2. Adam is aiming to improve the muscular endurance of his pectorals and biceps.

   Using a bar bell, he has a one rep max of 70 kg.

   Calculate the correct weight training limit for Adam and provide advice. [2]

   70 × 0.7 = 49 kg. Adam should lift a high number of reps[1] with no more than 49kg on the bar.[1]

CONSIDERATIONS TO PREVENT INJURY

In order to prevent injury, the training type and intensity should match the training purpose (e.g. aerobic or anaerobic).

A warm up should be completed

Warm ups gradually increase the oxygen going to the working muscles, increasing temperature and flexibility. Warm ups also raise the heart rate in preparation for exercise.

Appropriate clothing and footwear should be worn

Protective clothing, for example, supportive, shock-absorbing footwear, studs, shin pads or mouth guards can protect against injury and allow safe movement.

Hydration should be maintained

Drinking plenty of **fluids** replaces those lost in sport or training. This avoids dizziness and muscle cramps, and increases concentration.

Technique used should be correct, e.g. lifting technique

Poor technique can cause other body parts to compensate for a movement, putting too much strain on them, for example lifting and throwing. Tackling or contact sports also require the correct technique to avoid injury to either player involved.

Over training should be avoided, e.g. appropriate weight

Over training can result in fatigue, tedium or injury and could produce adaptations that are not in line with the fitness aims. Training intensity should always be matched to the individual so that it is challenging but manageable.

Taping/bracing should be used as necessary

Taping or **bracing** can be used to provide additional support and stabilisation for joints, muscles and tendons.

Stretches should not be overstretched or bounced

Static stretching is good for flexibility and warm ups but bouncing a stretch beyond its maximum can injure a muscle, causing tears and sprains.

Appropriate rest in between sessions to allow for recovery

Different types of sports, types of training or training programmes require varying levels of **rest** in between sessions to allow for full recovery from the stresses of intense exercise.

Explain how taping or bracing could lead to further injury.   [2]

Taping can mask an injury,[1] providing false confidence causing greater issues in the longer term.[1]

See **pages 15 and 49** for more details on the methods of recovery from vigorous exercise. These include cooling down, manipulation of diet, ice baths and massage.

HIGH ALTITUDE TRAINING

High altitude training is carried out over 2000 metres above sea level where the concentration of oxygen in the air is reduced. The body compensates by adapting, making more red blood cells to carry more oxygen.

Benefits of altitude training

- More red blood cells are produced which can carry more oxygen to the working muscles when training or playing sports at lower altitudes. This can help athletes perform more efficiently and for longer. They will be able to deliver oxygen more effectively, delay fatigue and work aerobically at higher intensities, which can provide a competitive advantage.

- Cardiovascular endurance is improved.

- Aerobic capacity is increased for a few weeks.

- Gaseous exchange becomes faster, enabling an athlete to work at a higher rate for a longer period.

- Benefits are maximised when performances are subsequently done at sea level where oxygen levels are highest.

Limitations of altitude training

- Detraining (**reversibility**) can occur as training sessions are more difficult with the lack of oxygen so athletes may not be able to train for as long or as intensely.

- Altitude sickness may prevent training for a few days until the athlete has adapted.

- Athletes may be affected by psychological issues associated with home sickness or unfamiliar surroundings which may cause them to underperfom, losing fitness.

- Benefits are short-lived.

Since altitude training is related to oxygen levels, it has little benefit on anaerobic performance.

For each of the different sports performers below, tick the appropriate column to indicate whether they would benefit or not from high altitude training. [3]

Sports performer	Benefit	No benefit
Tennis player		
Sprinter		
Marathon runner		

Tennis player – Benefit.[1]
Sprinter – No benefit.[1]
Marathon runner – Benefit.[1]

SEASONAL ASPECTS OF TRAINING

There are three distinct training seasons for performance athletes, each with their own characteristics.

Pre-season or preparation

Pre-season training involves **improving general fitness** to account for losses in the transition season. Any specific fitness needs or skills may be also be addressed in order to start the peak season at their best.

Competition, peak or playing season

The **competitive season** requires that **fitness levels are maintained** at their peak. Training sessions may also work on specific skills that can be brought into the next competition or match.

Specific types of training suited to the sport and individual can be introduced with varying intensities to replicate competitive conditions as closely as possible. Training may be tapered after pre-season training in order to conserve energy for key events.

Post-season or transition

Post-season training involves an opportunity for the body to **rest** with light levels of exercise (active rest) to maintain a level of general fitness before pre-season training starts again in earnest.

Which **one** of the following would be most suitable for a cricket player in their peak match season? [1]

A – Intense circuit and Fartlek training to build fitness, endurance and agility.

B – Skills and technique training with moderate fitness maintenance.

C – Active rest with light exercise.

D – Continuous training in the aerobic zone of maximum heart rate.

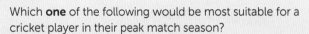

B. [1]

Remember that seasons change with the sport. They have nothing to do with the seasons of the year.

For example, football pre-season would start in July, peak season from August to May and post season in June.

EFFECTIVE USE OF WARM UP AND COOL DOWN

Warming up and cooling down routines significantly increase an athlete's ability to train to a higher level, to train more frequently, to avoid injury and to achieve better results.

Warming up

Warming up should include an activity that gradually raises the pulse, ready for exercise. Stretching the muscles increases pliability and flexibility, reducing the risk of injury. Sports related skills and drills are also commonly included.

This increases the amount of oxygen to the working muscles and provides mental preparation so that the athlete is ready for the main training session or competition.

Benefits of warming up include:

➕ The warming effect on body temperature

➕ The range of movement increased

➕ A gradual increase of effort to full pace to avoid physical or mental shock

➕ Psychological preparation

➕ The practice of physical skills through the whole range of movement

➕ Steps to reduce and prevent injury.

Cooling down

Cooling down requires maintaining an elevated breathing and heart rate by including a walk or jog, for example. Stretching allows muscles to lengthen whilst warm and then relax. A gradual reduction in intensity prevents overheating, light-headedness and nausea.

It also provides an opportunity to increase post exercise oxygen consumption (EPOC) to repay the oxygen debt, and encourages blood flow to return to the inactive organs and away from active muscles to prevent blood pooling.

Benefits of cooling down include:

➕ Allowing the body to recover

➕ The removal of lactic acid, CO_2 and waste products

➕ To reduce (delayed onset) muscle soreness (DOMS).

Explain why it is important to warm up before an intensive training session. [3]

Three from:
Gradually increase heart rate in preparation for exercise. [1]
Gradually increase blood flow around the body to warm muscles. [1]
Stretch and lengthen muscles to increase range of motion to prevent injury before stress. [1]
Increase oxygen flow to the working muscles in preparation for exercise. [1]
Prepare the mind for intense exercise and focus on training. [1]
Encourage blood flow to divert from the inactive organs to the active muscles. [1]

EXAMINATION PRACTICE 3

01 Which **one** of the following is **not** a type of strength? [1]

   ☐ A – Agile

   ☐ B – Explosive

   ☐ C – Maximal

   ☐ D – Static

02 In which of these sporting activities is reaction time most important? [1]

   ☐ A – Lawn bowls

   ☐ B – Motor racing

   ☐ C – Snooker

   ☐ D – Target shooting

03 A cricket player begins training more frequently. Which training principle are they using? [1]

   ☐ A – Specificity

   ☐ B – Progressive overload

   ☐ C – Reversibility

   ☐ D – Tedium

04 Jack is 16. Which **one** of the following is Jack's maximum heart rate? [1]

   ☐ A – 184

   ☐ B – 204

   ☐ C – 206

   ☐ D – 236

05 Explain how better health could help to improve fitness. [2]

06 Agility, balance, fast reaction time, strength and coordination are all useful components of fitness for a tennis player.

06.1 Name **one** other component of fitness useful to a tennis player.
Outline why this is important for a tennis player. [2]

06.2 Define coordination. Evaluate the importance of coordination for a tennis player. [4]

07 David and Elizabeth have been taking the Illinois Agility Test as part of their hockey club training.
They are both 16 years old. David's time was 17.1 seconds. Elizabeth's time was 17.2 seconds.
Analyse the data in table 1. What does it show about David and Elizabeth's performance and
level of agility? [3]

Performance category	Males aged 16–19 (sec)	Females aged 16–19 (sec)
Excellent	< 15.2	< 17.0
Good	15.2–16.1	17.0–17.9
Average	16.2–18.1	18.0–21.7
Fair	18.2–18.3	21.8–23.0
Poor	> 18.3	> 23.0

08   An outdoor activity centre offers rock climbing and kayaking. They have competitive teams for both sports that compete against people from other centres.

The centre trainer has decided to use a handgrip dynamometer test to measure the strength of competitors in both sports.

08.1 Describe how to carry out this test.   [3]

08.2 Evaluate whether the test is more relevant to a rock climber or a kayaker.   [6]

09   Dillon begins weight training but is unsure how to achieve the desired outcomes for his sport. Complete the table of advice by adding in each of the following components of fitness:

Muscular strength, Muscular endurance, Power

Component of fitness	Method
	Lift heavy weights, quickly
	Lift heavy weights, few times
	Lift light weights, many times

10   Callum is 16 year old football player representing his local team. He warms up well using stretching techniques and has read that plyometric training could be used to improve his performance.

10.1 State **three** factors other than stretching and warm-ups that Callum can use to help prevent injury in match play and training.   [3]

10.2 Discuss the appropriateness of plyometric training for Callum and any other factors he might consider to improve his performance.   [9]

11   High altitude training is used by long distance runners and games players.

11.1 Explain why high altitude training is less useful to anaerobic athletes.   [2]

11.2 Justify how high altitude training provides a competitive advantage to performers.   [4]

12   Warming up mentally prepares an athlete for a period of intense fitness and skills training.

Explain the physical effect on the body of warming up before training or exercise.   [2]

UNDERSTANDING HOW DATA IS COLLECTED

The collection of data is crucial to analysis and the formation of conclusions. How data is collected often depends on the type of data that is required.

Quantitative data

Quantitative data deals with numbers, and for that reason, it is more easily statistically analysed. Methods for collecting quantitative data commonly include **questionnaires** and **surveys**.

In a survey of 100 members of a local sports club, a questionnaire asked for the number of hours of exercise that respondents undertook each week. It also asked for their resting heart rate. Question 1 was segmented by hour to allow for easier analysis.

1. In the average week, how many hours of vigorous exercise do you complete?

| 0 | 1 | 2 | 3 | 4 | 5 | 6 | 7 | 8 | 9+ |

2. After a period of 20 mins after exercise, what is your resting heart rate in BPM?

64

Qualitative data

Qualitative data deals with descriptions. This includes opinions and emotions. **Interviews** and **observations** allow for more detailed and descriptive responses.

Whilst conducting the same survey, interviews with some members collected the following response to exercise patterns:

"I love running on cold mornings, but I tend not to bother if it is raining."

Observations can be used to judge human behaviour over time to find patterns. The manager of the sports club observed that sports club members tended to change their use over time.

"A lot of people have high levels of exercise in January but that quickly tails off until the summer when longer evenings bring more people outside."

See **page 37** for more detail and definitions on quantitative and qualitative data.

PRESENTING DATA

Data can be presented in graphical formats to show patterns more clearly.

Presenting data in tables

The data collected from the sports club survey can be tallied and averaged in a **table**:

Exercise hours per week	Frequency	Average resting heart rate
0	3	78
1	16	75
2	**24**	**72**
3	17	68
4	12	69
5	10	66
6	8	65
7	3	63
8	5	61
9	2	57

24 people exercised for 2 hours per week

Plotting basic bar charts and line graphs

Using the data in the table above, a **bar chart** (figure 1) can be plotted to show the number of people that exercise for 0–9 hours per week. A **line graph** (figure 2) can be plotted to show the average heart rate for club members for each level of exercise.

Figure 1: Bar chart

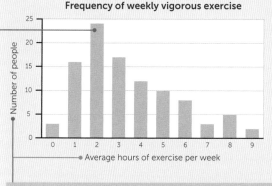

Figure 2: Line graph

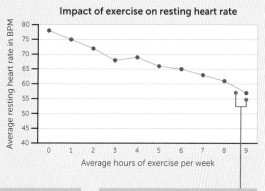

Always label the x and **y** axes on charts and graphs for full marks. Axis labels should include the units, for example: people, BPM or weeks.

Mark each point on a line graph, then join the markers.

Look at the line graph in Figure 2. Suggest the relationship between resting heart rate and hours of exercise in this sample of people. [1]

Those who did greater amounts of weekly exercise had lower resting heart rates.[1]

ANALYSIS AND EVALUATION OF DATA

Once data has been collected, it can be analysed, graphed and then interpreted. An evaluation of the data can more easily be made after this process.

Interpreting tabular data

The data in the table below shows the number of medals won by the GBR team in the Summer Olympics since 1992. Without some analysis, data tables can be difficult to interpret.

Medals	Barcelona 1992	Atlanta 1996	Sydney 2000	Athens 2004	Beijing 2008	London 2012	Rio 2016	Tokyo 2021
Gold	5	1	11	9	19	29	27	22
Silver	3	8	10	9	13	18	23	20
Bronze	12	6	7	12	19	18	17	22

This data could be analysed, for example, by sorting or by finding the totals for each year:

Total	20	15	28	30	51	65	67	64

Figure 1: GBR Summer Olympic medals since 1992

1. From the table of data presented in Figure 1, identify the most successful year for the GBR team in terms of gold medals won. [1]

2012.[1]

Interpreting graphical data

Bar charts

Data presented graphically is often clearer and easier to extract useful information from.

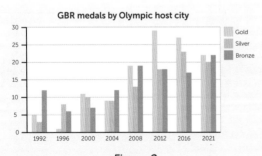

Figure 2

2. Look at the bar chart presented in Figure 2. Suggest **two** possible reasons why the performance of GBR athletes improved after 1996. [2]

(National Lottery) funding was diverted into elite sport in 1996.[1] A new high-performance system spread across UK sports, putting the concept of marginal gains at the heart of training.[1] New, raw talent was better nurtured.[1] Team spirit increased in Beijing 2008 and the winning feeling has increased confidence and pride in athletes and their performance directors.[1]

⋅⋅⋅ Interpreting graphical data continued

Line graphs

Line graphs are often useful to see **trends** within the data. A trendline can also be added.

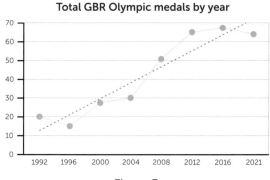

Figure 3

3. From the line graph presented in Figure 3, suggest the number of GBR medals likely in 2024.
Give a reason for your estimate. [2]

60–70[1] medals based on a plateau since 2012.[1] / 70–85[1] based on the trend line.[1]

Pie charts

Pie charts are used to show the proportions of a whole. In analysing charts, it is often helpful to look for **patterns**, **similarities** and **differences** by **comparing** sets of information. For example, two data points on a graph could be compared, or two points in time.

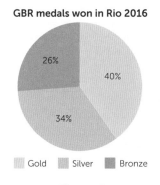

Figure 4

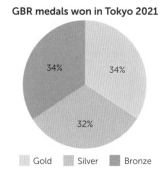

Figure 5

4. Look at Figures 4 and 5. Analyse the performance of the GBR team in both years. [2]

The proportion of silver medals remained at roughly a third.[1] Bronze medals increased in 2021 whilst gold medals decreased / potential gold or silver medallists may have lost out to gain a silver or bronze instead.[1] Performance was roughly consistent from one year to the next.[1]

Make comparisons where possible and draw conclusions from data using the information provided and your own knowledge.

EXAMINATION PRACTICE 4

01 Which **one** of the following is an example of qualitative data?   [1]
  ☐ A – The Austrian skier has won five previous world champion slalom events
  ☐ B – His split time was slower in the middle section by +0.42
  ☐ C – The Austrian skier looks uncomfortable at the moment
  ☐ D – He placed fourth in this race

02 Figure 1 shows a table containing the number of yellow cards handed out over six seasons for Windham Athletic football team.

Season	2017/18	2018/19	2019/20	2020/21	2021/22	2022/23
Yellow cards	58	71	49	44	42	41

Figure 1

02.1 Draw a bar chart using the graph paper below and the data provided in Figure 1. Interpret the data in Figure 1.   [2]

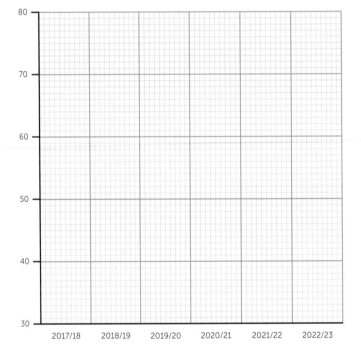

02.2 Identify **one** piece of outlying or anomalous data from the series.   [1]

02.3 Identify the trend shown in the data.   [1]

02.4 Suggest **two** reasons for the trend.   [2]

02.5 Suggest what the number of yellow cards is likely to be for the 2023/24 season.   [1]

TOPICS FOR PAPER 2
Socio-cultural influences and well-being in physical activity and sport

Information about Paper 2

Mandatory written exam: 1 hour 15 minutes
Externally assessed.
78 marks
All questions are mandatory
30% of the qualification grade
Calculators are permitted in this examination.

Specification coverage

Sports psychology, socio-cultural influences, health, fitness and well-being, and the use of data.

The content for this assessment will be drawn from topics 3.2.1 to 3.2.3 of the specification.

Questions

The paper will consist of a mixture of multiple choice/objective test questions, short answer questions and extended answer questions.

CLASSIFICATION OF SKILLS

Different sports require different sets of skills for performers to acquire and perfect.

Skill and ability

A **skill** is a learned action or learned behaviour with the intention of bringing about predetermined results, with maximum certainty and minimum outlay of time and energy.

An **ability** is an inherited, stable trait that determines an individual's potential to learn or acquire a skill.

Skills classifications are continuums. A skill may lie somewhere on a line between one extreme and the other. You may need to justify why a skill is nearer one end than another, e.g:

Classifications of skill

Skills can be classified in any of four ways:

Basic or complex

A **basic skill** (e.g. jogging) requires few decisions to be made that affect the skill so they are learned quickly and require a low level of coordination or concentration to complete.

A **complex skill** (e.g. high jump) requires lots of decisions in order to be successful and requires a high level of coordination and concentration.

Self-paced or externally paced

A **self-paced skill** (e.g. tennis serve) is started when the performer decides to start it. The speed, rate or pace of the skill is controlled by the performer.

An **externally-paced skill** (e.g. sprint start) is started because of an external factor. The speed, rate or pace of the skill is controlled by external factors, for example, an opponent.

Gross or fine

Gross skills (e.g. javelin throw) use large muscles or muscle groups to perform big, strong, powerful movements.

Fine skills (e.g. golf putt) are responsible for small and precise movement, requiring high levels of accuracy and coordination. Fine skills involve the use of a small group of muscles.

Open or closed

An **open skill** (e.g. football tackle) is performed in a certain way to deal with a changing or unstable environment, e.g. to outwit an opponent.

A **closed skill** (e.g. platform dive) is one which is not affected by the environment or performers within it. The skill tends to be done the same way each time.

Justify the skill of bowling a cricket bowl using each of the classifications above. [4]

Complex as it requires making decisions about the type and placement of the ball with several movements involved in the run-up and swing.[1]

Closed as it is performed the same way each time.[1]
Accept open as it may depend on the batsman's stance, condition and style.

Self-paced as the speed and pace of the ball is controlled by the bowler.[1]

Gross as it involves big movements of the arm and body.[1] Accept that fine movements are involved by the fingers to control the ball / spin / to precisely hit the stumps.

GOAL SETTING

Sporting goals vary according to what the performer wants to achieve. Goals can be set by athletes themselves or by their coaches. They provide motivation and something measurable to aim for.

Goal types

Performance goals

Performance goals are driven by personal achievement. Performers compare themselves against what they have already done or suggest what they are going to do. They have no social comparison such as the results of teammates, opponents or national records. A personal best is a performance goal.

Beginners tend to set themselves performance goals as it may demotivate them to compare themselves to more successful performers so early in their own training or sports career. Winning at this stage may be an unrealistic goal and failure can put them off.

Outcome goals

Outcome goals are set based on specific desired results, for example, winning. However, setting outcome goals can be highly demotivating as the athlete cannot control the outcome of other athletes which may affect the success of their own goal.

It is generally accepted that outcome goals should be avoided as they rely on factors that cannot be controlled, e.g. other performers.

Combining goals

Elite level athletes strive to win. Outcome goals are everything, but they commonly combine performance goals (for example, to increase their shot percentage in basketball) with outcome goals to hone smaller parts of their performance in order to get the desired outcome (a greater contribution to a team win).

Jessica is aiming for a personal best this track season. Explain whether this is a performance or outcome goal. [2]

Performance goal[1] because it does not involve comparison with others.[1]

SMART TARGETS

SMART targets are appropriately defined goals that can be used to improve and/or optimise performance.

SMART targets of goal setting are:

S   Specific

Goals must be specific to the demands of the sport, the muscles or the movements used.

M   Measurable

It must be possible to measure whether a goal has been met.

A   Accepted

A goal must be accepted by the performer and others involved, e.g. a coach.

R   Realistic

Goals should actually be possible to complete / within capability.

T   Time-bound

A set period of time or deadline by which the goal will be achieved.

Nina says she wants to improve her golf handicap. Identify **one** way in which she can make this goal SMART. [1]

Measurable – Nina needs to state how many points she wants to reduce her handicap by / or give a target handicap.[1]
Realistic – Nina needs to be confident that she is capable of reaching her goal in the time given.[1]
Time bound – Nina needs to state a date by when the goal should be met.[1] The goal is already specific.

Beginner skier

S   I will learn to link turns using parallel skis in the traverse.

M   I will ski for four hours each day, for one week.

A   My instructor and I agree that I can do it.

R   This is what people are expected to do in one week.

T   I will achieve it by the end of the week.

Downhill racer

S   Improve my start time by keeping my poles nearer my feet for a faster split in the top section.

M   I will shave off an average 0.6s from my first split time.

A   The coach says I am capable and I am getting better.

R   A good start can improve a race time by up to 2s so this is possible.

T   I will achieve it in 28 days of practice.

BASIC INFORMATION PROCESSING

The information processing model conveys the process through which decisions are made in sport about how best to react in different situations.

Basic information processing model

Each stage of the model explains the function of the brain and its sensory response to a situation.

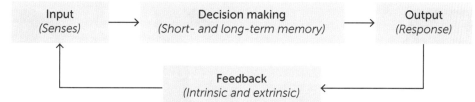

Example

Input

The player will take information from their environment via their senses, for example sight, sound and touch. They will see the ball being struck and coming towards them.

They will choose the most relevant information from the display to focus on (the ball flying through the air) and block out irrelevant information (for example, the crowd). This is called **selective attention**.

Decision-making

The player can make a decision using **short-term memory** if they have made a similar decision in the last few seconds. Otherwise, the player uses **long-term memory** to see if they have experienced the situation before by comparing it with their short-term memory observations of the curve of the ball, its pace, spin and direction.

They can then select an appropriate response using this information, for example by repositioning themselves around other players and to get under the ball.

Output

The decision is sent to the appropriate muscles in the arms, legs and neck to carry out the response (for example a jump and header).

Explain what happens at the feedback stage of the information processing model in response to a football header attempt on goal, following a corner kick. [2]

Feedback – Information is received extrinsically (from others) if the header / interception was successful or not based on whether a goal was scored directly or indirectly.[1] Information can be provided by the manager or captain who may point out if the technique was correct in the circumstances or needs to be changed.[1] Information is received intrinsically (from themself) / kinaesthetically (by touch) as to how the shot felt leaving the head.[1]

GUIDANCE ON PERFORMANCE

Coaches need to identify the most appropriate methods to provide guidance to beginners and elite level performers.

Types of guidance

Visual (seeing)	**Verbal** (hearing)
A golf instructor demonstrates the correct stance and setup posture.	*A sports team huddles to listen to verbal guidance from their coach.*

Visual guidance includes watching an instructor, video footage, images or diagrams.

- ➕ Quick and concise which is especially good for beginners so they can create a mental picture to copy
- ➕ Slow motion replays can be used for detailed analysis of complex skills
- ➖ Complex skills can be difficult to demonstrate clearly
- ➖ Performers need to be paying attention.

Explanations of how to do things, or audible cues on when to move or hold a position.

- ➕ Can be provided whilst a sporting action is being performed
- ➕ Easily combined with other forms of guidance
- ➖ Less suitable for beginners if technical language is used
- ➖ Complex skills are difficult to explain in words.

Manual (Physical assistance with movement)

A gymnastics trainer physically corrects positioning on the parallel bars.

Coaches may physically move parts of the body into the correct position, stance or through a complete range of motion.

➕ Useful for beginners to get the feel of a movement or position, or for safety

➕ Subtle positioning can be adjusted to develop complex skills

➖ Useful on an individual basis only rather than with sports teams

➖ Less suitable for elite performers

➖ Physical contact requires consent.

Mechanical (use of objects or aids)

A trampolinist using a mechanical harness in practice.

Sports equipment is used to assist the performer, for example, swimming paddles, pull buoy floats or tennis ball machines.

➕ Useful for beginners to feel the motion, technique or for safety

➕ Builds confidence without the fear of injury

➖ Performers may come to rely on the support

➖ Mistakes in technique using the aids can become engrained.

A rowing coach needs to provide guidance to an elite coxless four whilst on the water.
Evaluate the most suitable type of guidance.   [3]

Verbal[1] as the guidance may require technical language[1] / it can be given whilst the crew are moving[1] / visual and manual or mechanical methods are less helpful to elite performers[1] and not relevant to this situation.[1]

FEEDBACK ON PERFORMANCE

Beginners and elite athletes have different requirements when it comes to feedback on their performances.

Types of feedback

● Better for beginners   ● Better for elite performers

Positive feedback – Explains what a performer is doing right, e.g. *"Excellent follow through"*.

Appropriateness for beginners – Essential for motivation when performances aren't consistently good, but it could give a false picture of actual performance.

Appropriateness for elite performers – Provides confidence and reassurance.

Knowledge of results – Provides feedback on the outcome, for example *% first serves in, score, time or distance*.

Appropriateness for beginners – Useful as a quick measure of success. Knowing the result builds confidence in progress.

Appropriateness for elite performers – Commonly evident to elite performers, for example the percentage pass rate for top flight footballers.

Negative feedback – Explains what a performer is doing wrong e.g. *"Keep your chin tucked in"*.

Appropriateness for beginners – Can be demoralising for some beginners.

Appropriateness for elite performers – Commonly used to focus more efficiently on precisely what to improve.

Knowledge of performance – Focuses on individual elements of a performance, for example, *grip, stance, start* or *follow through*.

Appropriateness for beginners – Can be detailed so it is often simplified for beginners.

Appropriateness for elite performers – Helps to fine tune elements of a performance.

Extrinsic feedback – Is provided by an outside observer, commonly a coach.

Appropriateness for beginners – Beginners are less aware of what a successful technique looks like or feels like, and they don't know how to improve their technique.

Appropriateness for elite performers – Elite performers may combine extrinsic and intrinsic feedback.

Intrinsic (or kinaesthetic) feedback – Comes from within. It is 'felt' by the performer through their own senses or muscles.

Appropriateness for beginners – Beginners do not usually have enough experience to have developed a feeling for the correct technique.

Appropriateness for elite performers – Elite athletes have a strongly developed sense of their own performance.

Dana is a competitive weight lifter. She uses a wall mirror when she is training to gain feedback. Explain why an athlete may use a wall mirror to gain feedback.   [3]

A mirror provides an instant knowledge of performance[1] which helps to develop / fine tune technique.[1] Extrinsic feedback from the mirror[1] can help to develop / fine tune intrinsic feedback.[1]

AROUSAL AND THE INVERTED-U THEORY

Arousal is defined as a physical and mental (physiological and psychological) state of alertness or readiness, varying from deep sleep to intense excitement and alertness.

Inverted-U theory

The **inverted-U theory** graph shows the relationship between **arousal** and **performance**.

When under aroused, performance levels are low as the athlete may get bored and lose focus. As arousal increases, so does performance until it reaches an optimum zone. As arousal increases further, stress levels build and a state of **over arousal** is reached, causing performance levels to decrease again.

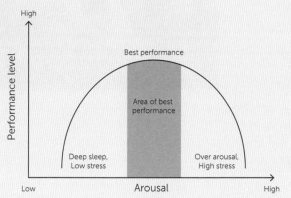

> ⭐ When discussing the link between arousal levels and performance levels, refer to skills and not the sport e.g. a rugby tackle and not rugby.

How optimal arousal levels vary according to skills

Depending on the skill being performed, the placement of the graph along the **x** axis (arousal) will vary. Sporting actions that involve **gross motor skills** (e.g. a rugby tackle) generally require a higher **state of arousal**. **Fine motor skills** (e.g. a golf putt) commonly involve **lower levels of arousal**.

An inverted-U graph for two skills is shown below.

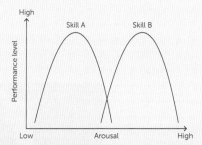

Suggest a different sporting skill for Skill A and Skill B. Justify each answer. [4]

Skill A: Snooker break, darts throw, golf putt, table tennis serve[1] as the optimal arousal level is low for a fine skill.[1] Skill B: Football/rugby tackle, amateur boxing punch, scull in rowing, lifting a heavy weight[1] as the optimal arousal level is high for gross movements.[1]

USING STRESS MANAGEMENT TECHNIQUES TO CONTROL AROUSAL LEVELS

Before and during a sporting performance, athletes use a variety of techniques to help control their levels of arousal.

Deep breathing

Performers exaggerate their breaths in and out to reduce stress, increase oxygen to the brain to help concentration and to restore or maintain a calm rhythm to their breathing.

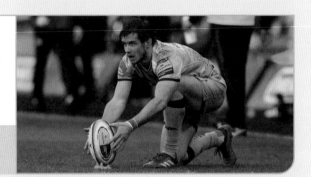

A rugby player calms himself before a conversion kick.

Positive self-talk

Self-talk is a psychological technique involving the performer giving themselves instructions and words of encouragement in their head.

For example, a basketball player taking a free throw shot to win a game may think *'I'm going to score this shot'*. This creates positivity.

Mental rehearsal, visualisation or imagery

By mentally picturing themselves performing a skill perfectly and imagining positive outcomes before attempting it (such as a podium finish), sportspeople can relax and focus on their performance. This is a common technique used by field athletes such as long- and high-jumpers, football players before a penalty kick, or divers before leaving the platform.

Visualisation and imagery can also be used to imagine being in a calm, relaxing environment, blocking out the noise and pressure from a large audience for example.

A Belgian athlete mentally rehearsing the women's heptathlon shot put.

A swimmer using visualisation before the start of the men's 50m backstroke.

DIRECT AND INDIRECT AGGRESSION

Aggression in its raw form is a deliberate intent to harm or injure another person, which can be physical or mental. In sport, the use of the term is more defined, as aggression takes different forms.

Performers must ensure that any acts of aggression are within the rules of their sport. Direct and indirect aggression can be used to intimidate the opposition – which isn't always permitted.

Direct aggression

Direct aggression is an act which involves **physical contact** with others, for example, a rugby tackle or amateur boxing punch. A deliberate late football tackle, elbow or push, for example, may be attempted but would constitute a foul if seen by the referee.

Indirect aggression

Indirect aggression is taken out on an **object** to gain advantage, for example hitting a tennis ball hard during a rally. Indirect aggression may be within the rules of a game or it may be considered unsportsmanlike.

Figure 1: A rugby tackle during an England v Scotland match at the 2023 Guinness 6 Nations match at Twickenham.

Using Figure 1, explain the type of aggression shown in the behaviour of the players. [2]

Direct aggression[1] because they are making deliberate physical contact[1] with each other.

INTROVERTS AND EXTROVERTS

Different people have different personality types which can suit some sports better than others.

Introverts	Extroverts

Introverts tend to be **shy** and **quiet**, **thoughtful** and enjoy **being on their own**.

They tend to prefer **individual sports** that:

- require a **high level of concentration or precision**,
- use **fine skills**,
- require **low arousal**.

Extroverts tend to enjoy interaction with others and are **sociable**. They are **enthusiastic** and talkative, but **prone to boredom** when left on their own.

They tend to prefer **team sports** where:

- there is a **fast pace**,
- **gross movement skills** are required,
- **lower levels of concentration** are needed.

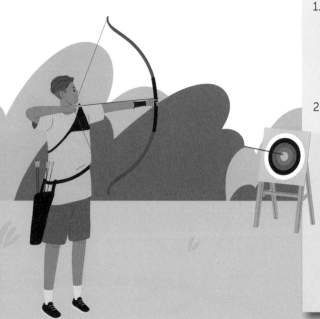

1. Which **one** of the following sports would be most suited to an introvert? [1]

   A: Cricket
   B: Ice hockey
   C: Platform diving
   D: Volleyball

2. Give **two** reasons why some long distance runners like to train on their own. [2]

   1. *C: Platform diving.[1]*
   2. *Solo running is an individual sport which they may prefer if they are introverted.[1] They could be running for several hours so need to be comfortable being on their own.[1] Maintaining an activity for long periods requires high levels of concentration.[1] There is no requirement to socialise with others which introverts prefer.[1] Running is a low arousal activity which most suits introverts.[1]*

INTRINSIC AND EXTRINSIC MOTIVATION

Motivation is the drive to succeed or the desire to achieve something, or to be inspired to do something. This can be intrinsic or extrinsic.

Intrinsic motivation

Intrinsic motivation comes from **within**. People are intrinsically motivated if they want to feel a sense of **pride**, **satisfaction**, **accomplishment** or **self-worth**.

Achieving a personal best is an intrinsically motivated achievement.

Extrinsic motivation

Extrinsic motivation is driven by **external sources**. These can be tangible or intangible:

- **Tangible factors** include prizes, for example, **certificates**, **trophies**, **medals** or **money**
- **Intangible factors** include the need to perform well to receive **praise**, **feedback** or **applause**.

Striving for gold in the Olympics is an extrinsic factor in motivation.

The merits of intrinsic and extrinsic motivation in sport

Intrinsic motivation is generally deemed more effective as it is always within you, and more likely to lead to continued or sustained effort and participation.

Performers can become over-reliant on extrinsic factors. Extrinsic rewards may result in feelings of pride and self-satisfaction, but these feelings may be short-lived. An overuse of extrinsic factors, especially if they aren't achieved, can undermine the strength of your own intrinsic motivation.

Explain why a beginner may find intrinsic motivation more valuable than extrinsic motivation. [2]

A beginner may make a lot of mistakes which requires internal motivation to overcome through continued practice.[1] Intrinsic motivation encourages beginners to play sport for enjoyment rather than for prizes which are less likely to come in the early stages of learning.[1] / Extrinsic motivation may fade if rewards are not gained and lead to giving up the sport.[1]

EXAMINATION PRACTICE 5

01 Which **one** of the following describes knowledge of performance? [1]
- ☐ A – Feedback about the technique used
- ☐ B – Feedback about whether the performer won or not
- ☐ C – Feedback that focuses entirely on what was wrong
- ☐ D – Information received from within the performer

02 Which **one** of the following is an example of manual guidance? [1]
- ☐ A – Having your hips and body mass moved over the downhill ski by an instructor
- ☐ B – Listening to the football manager in a half time talk
- ☐ C – Using swimming paddles to develop a cleaner and more powerful technique
- ☐ D – Watching a coach perform a defensive shot in cricket

03 Which **one** of the following skills requires a high level of arousal for optimum performance? [1]
- ☐ A – Jumping a hurdle in sprinting
- ☐ B – Pistol shooting
- ☐ C – Putting a ball in golf
- ☐ D – Shooting a bow in archery

04 Which **one** of the following is an example of direct aggression? [1]
- ☐ A – Conversion in rugby
- ☐ B – Drive in golf
- ☐ C – Shoulder barge in football
- ☐ D – Smash in volleyball

05 Which **one** of the following is a characteristic of an introvert? [1]
- ☐ A – Enthusiastic
- ☐ B – Shy
- ☐ C – Sociable
- ☐ D – Talkative

06 Give **one** sporting example of an open skill. Justify your answer. [3]

07 Jo has started badminton with the hope of playing for her local team one day. Her instructor has provided a performance goal to help her improve her accuracy and to perfect specific movements in gameplay.

Jo has committed a number of unforced errors (errors when she was in full control and not under pressure) and has set herself a target to achieve.

Jo has committed the following percentage of unforced errors in recent matches:

Match	1	2	3	Target
Unforced errors	39%	34%	32%	15%

Table 1

07.1 Explain why the instructor has provided a performance goal to help motivate Jo. [2]

07.2 Analyse the data in table 1. Identify **two** ways in which Jo can make her target percentage of errors SMART. [2]

08 Look at **Figure 2**.

Figure 2

08.1 Complete the basic information processing model diagram by adding in the missing stages. [3]

08.2 Using a skill from a named sport, explain what happens at the input stage of the model. [2]

09 Rugby players commonly use stress management techniques to optimise their performance.

09.1 Draw an inverted-U graph representing the skill of taking a rugby conversion. [4]

09.2 Identify and describe **one** stress management technique that could be used by a player preparing to take a conversion. [2]

10 Evaluate the effectiveness of intrinsic motivation for an elite performer in sport. [4]

ENGAGEMENT PATTERNS OF DIFFERENT SOCIAL GROUPS AND THE FACTORS AFFECTING PARTICIPATION

Engagement patterns refer to the common trend that is seen in a social group when looking at how much they engage and participate in exercise and activity.

Social grouping by   Gender

Examples of factors affecting participation:

Sexism

Sexist or **stereotypical** attitudes may affect how comfortable (or not) women feel about taking part. Most sports clubs now cater for both men and women, but some can still be largely male dominated, e.g. golf clubs.

Role models

There may be a lack of gender specific role models to inspire others of that gender to participate.

Accessibility

Regular sports teams for women may not always exist within a convenient travelling distance.

An England player during the FIFA Women's World Cup.

Media coverage

Media coverage may be more prevalent for males, compared to females.

---

1. Males are more likely to participate in sports than females. Identify **three** reasons why female participation numbers are typically below those of males. [3]

2. Calculate the percentage difference in participation between males and females. Use the data provided in Figure 1. [1]

   1. *Females are less likely to take part in competitive sport.[1] Some sports are stereotypically more male oriented e.g. boxing.[1] Less funding / sponsorship available for females.[1] Discrimination / sexism in some sports.[1] Lack of female role models / less media coverage of female sports people.[1] Pregnancy / menstruation may prevent participation.[1] Childcare may be difficult to find in order to create time for sport.[1] Lack of female sports clubs / teams locally.[1]*
   2. *63.1 – 59.8 = 3.3%.[1]*

Figure 1: Sport England, November 2021.

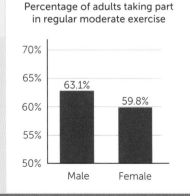

Percentage of adults taking part in regular moderate exercise

Male 63.1%   Female 59.8%

Social grouping by Race, religion and culture

Examples of factors affecting participation:

Culture and religion

Certain religions require specific clothing or commitments that may make participation harder to achieve, for example **fasting**.

Role models

There may be a lack of cultural role models for others to aspire to.

Attitudes

Racism by other sportspeople or spectators can affect people's decision to participate in a sport, and can negatively influence a team coach's decisions.

Some religious discrimination may prevent performers from wearing a hijab, or finding swimming hats to accommodate natural black hair, for example. **Homophobia** or **transphobia** may also negatively impact participation in sport.

Inclusiveness

It may be perceived that not all activities are inclusive for those from different cultural backgrounds.

Familiarity

Sporting opportunities may be far more widespread now than in the past, but if these remain unfamiliar to people, they are less likely to get involved.

As of 2022, the UK Chief Medical Officers' Guidelines recommend that adults should get at least 150 minutes of moderate physical activity per week. Children and young people aged 5–18 should aim to do 60 minutes of activity each day.

Moderate activity means something that raises the heart and breathing rate. This includes walking, cycling and PE classes.

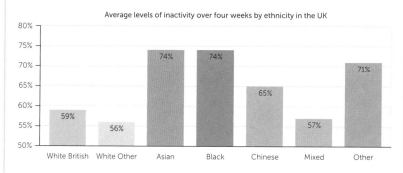

Average levels of inactivity over four weeks by ethnicity in the UK

- White British: 59%
- White Other: 56%
- Asian: 74%
- Black: 74%
- Chinese: 65%
- Mixed: 57%
- Other: 71%

Figure 2: Sport England, November 2021

As there are so many factors that can affect participation rates it is often a good idea to come up with an acronym to remember some of these- e.g., FARCE. 'It is a FARCE that more people are not influenced to engage in participation.'

Family influences, **A**ccessibility, **R**ole models, **C**ost, **E**ducation.

Social grouping by   Age

Examples of factors affecting participation:

Socio-economic factors

Younger people may not have the money to afford to take part in certain activities. Older people may have increased financial commitments and living costs that lower their **disposable income** available for sport.

Education

Time for schoolwork may come before time for evening sports clubs. Some schools offer greater sporting provision than others. People may simply not know what is available to them.

Accessibility

Not all clubs and memberships are available to all **ages** - some may not allow children.

Media coverage

An increase in media coverage of older sports performers may motivate older people to take part. Most active sports people disappear from the media when they retire, which is usually only in their 30s.

Available leisure time

As people age, they may take on more commitments, work shifts or increase their working hours to the point that they have less time for exercise.

---

3. The adult participation in sporting activities for different age groups is shown in Figure 3.
   Give **two** reasons why the over 75s have significantly lower levels of participation. [2]

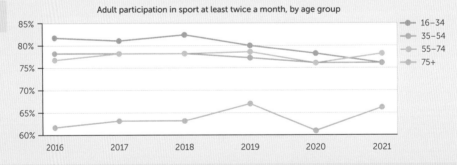

Figure 3

Answers may include: Illness / obesity / poor health,[1] poor mobility,[1] friends or social group do not participate,[1] lack of older role models,[1] self conscious / feel too old,[1] fear of injury,[1] lack of elderly sports groups / provision,[1] discrimination against the elderly.[1]

Most of the factors that affect participation can be related to any of the social groups.
For example: more media coverage, an increase in positive role models, improved education or an increase in leisure time can all positively affect the participation rates of all of the social groups.

Social grouping by   Family

Examples of factors affecting participation:

Role models

Active parents are more likely to have active children. They are positive role models in this respect and children will often become interested in those sports that other family members participate in.

Family commitments

When adults start a family, childcare or children's activities often become a priority over their own exercise needs. This commonly reduces the amount of time for exercise in the 25–55 age groups.

Jobs often demand more time as people become more experienced or senior in their roles.

Education

Some families may not know what is available to them in their local area.

People from lower socio-economic groups are less likely to participate in regular activity than those from higher socio-economic backgrounds.

Social grouping by   Disability

Examples of factors affecting participation:

Role models

There may be a lack of disabled role models to inspire disabled performers.

Boccia, Rio 2016 Paralympic Games.

Accessibility

Some facilities may not have suitable access for wheelchair users.

Discrimination

Some performers may feel that there is a negative **stereotype** towards those with a disability.

Media coverage

Despite increased media coverage of para sports, it is still a small fraction compared to that of mainstream sports.

4. Explain how **two** named factors can negatively affect the participation rate of disabled people.   [4]

Any two named factors with explanation: Factor: access[1] as some sports facilities do not cater for the accessibility requirements of all disabilities.[1] Factor: role models.[1] When there are only a few disabled role models, they are less able to act as an inspiration for other people with a disability to take part.[1] Factor: adaptability.[1] Some facilities may not offer adapted sports to include all disabilities. [1] Factor: stereotyping.[1] There may be a stereotype that disabled users are unable to participate.[1]

COMMERCIALISATION OF PHYSICAL ACTIVITY AND SPORT

Commercialisation is to manage or to exploit (an organisation or activity) in a way designed to make profit. This involves **sponsorship** and **media** coverage.

The golden triangle

1 The media (usually television) pays money to the sport to be able to film and broadcast the event(s).

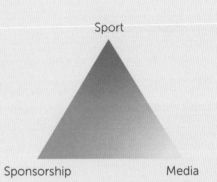

Sport

Sponsorship   Media

2 The media, for example Sky Sports, Amazon Prime or BT Sport, provides sports coverage to gain revenue from viewer subscriptions.

3 Companies pay money to the sport to sponsor an event

4 Sporting organisations receive valuable funding and income from sponsors and the media which can be invested in areas such as grass roots sport, stadia or elite athlete development.

5 By sponsoring the event, sponsors increase their publicity and brand awareness which they hope will boost sales of their products and services, increasing their profit by more than the cost of sponsorship.

1. Explain the relationship between sport, media and sponsorship. [2]
2. Explain how commercialisation could have a negative impact on sport. [2]

  1. *Any two from: Sport receives money from sponsors and from the media.[1] Sponsors can showcase their brand to increase their profit via the media.[1] The media gain money from subscribers who want to watch the sport on television.[1]*

  2. *External funding can be relied upon and withdrawn at no notice as they do not want to be associated with poor performance, injury or misbehaviour.[1] Minority sports / groups rarely attract enough attention to engage major sponsorship as the sponsors want large audiences[1] which means these sports continue to struggle in terms of their own funding and promotion / women's football clubs are paid only a fraction of the sponsorship compared to men's clubs.[1]*

TYPES OF SPONSORSHIP AND THE MEDIA

Sponsorship is the provision of funds or other forms of support to an individual or event for some commercial return, i.e. profit. Sponsorship can be provided in a variety of ways and is advertised and promoted through the media.

You may be required to simply state the types of sponsorship or the types of media.

However, be careful as you may be required to give more of a description (characteristics) or even an explanation (purposes / reasons).

Types of sponsorship

Financial (Giving money or financial assistance.)

London Marathon has been part funded by sponsor Lucozade Sport.

Equipment (E.g. golf clubs or cricket bats.)

A tennis player with sponsored equipment.

Clothing, **footwear** and **branded kit**.

England's Rugby kit has been sponsored by Umbro and O_2.

Facilities (Naming rights for stadia.)

Emirates stadium of Arsenal FC, London.

Types of media

 Television   Social media   (Printed) Press

Radio   Internet

1. State **three** types of sponsorship. [3]
2. Describe how **two** named types of media can be used to broadcast sport. [4]

---

1. *Any three from: Financial,[1] clothing / footwear,[1] equipment,[1] or facilities.[1]*
2. *Any two named media types with explanation. Television[1] can be live or via a highlights programme.[1] Radio[1] can be free to air such as BBC 5 live.[1] Social media[1] accounts can be updated 24/7 to provide information, facts and opinions.[1] Internet.[1] Fan and club websites can update the public on all matters relating to the sports club.[1]*

POSITIVE AND NEGATIVE IMPACTS OF SPONSORSHIP AND THE MEDIA

Sponsorship influences the commercialisation of physical activity and sport through a variety of ways.

Positive and negative impacts

Performer

A golfer is sponsored by Nike.

- ⊕ Clothing: Performers receive free or subsidised clothing to wear from the sponsor.
- ⊕ Equipment: Free access to the highest quality equipment.
- ⊕ Facilities: Use of high-quality facilities to train or compete in.
- ⊕ Profile: Coverage in the media can bring fame and allow them to ask for more money. They may also get the chance to earn from product endorsements.
- ⊖ Sponsor demands: Required to attend sponsorship events which may conflict with training schedules.
- ⊖ Equipment: Sponsor may insist that they use certain equipment or clothing that they are not comfortable with.
- ⊖ Pressure: Media attention increases the pressure to perform and can demand interviews, which would reduce enjoyment.
- ⊖ Reputation: Media can easily damage the reputation of a performer.

Sport

Women's football Wales v England, World Cup Qualifier

- ⊕ Interest: Interest in the sport will grow because of media coverage / more role models are created.
- ⊕ Competitions: There may be more competitions held.
- ⊕ Income: The sport will earn more money from sponsorship and media coverage. This money can be spent on grass roots sport, larger prize pots, coaching, development, and facilities.
- ⊕ Education: Media coverage will inform the public about the sport.
- ⊕ Facilities: Better or bigger facilities can be built.
- ⊖ Scandals: Reputational damage if scandals are publicised in the media, e.g. match fixing.
- ⊖ Attachment: Sport may get attached to an undesirable sponsor.
- ⊖ Reliance: The sport may become too reliant on sponsor / media money.
- ⊖ Start times: Start times maybe dictated by the media.

Justify why sponsorship and media coverage can be positive for sports performers. [3]

Any three from: Access to state-of-the-art equipment which can enhance performance / help subsidise costs.[1] Provision of free and/or performance-enhancing clothing.[1] Use of high-quality facilities to train at / access to top coaches.[1] Higher profile within the media, giving access to product endorsement / further sponsorship / more money.[1]

Officials

FIFA match official using a headset.

- ⊕ Profile: Officials will gain a higher profile in the media and can command a higher wage.
- ⊕ Sponsorship: Officials may be sponsored and gain more money to access better equipment.
- ⊕ Media: Media technology is used to assist with decision making.
- ⊖ Over-reliance: Officials may become over-reliant on media devices to make decisions.
- ⊖ Reputation: Reputational damage when incorrect decisions are exposed.
- ⊖ Pressure: May be more accountable in the media for their decisions.

Audience / spectator

Home viewing of sport.

- ⊕ 24/7 coverage: Spectators can gain access to 24/7 news and coverage through the media.
- ⊕ Education: Spectators can be educated through media channels.
- ⊕ Better viewing experience: Action replays / slow-motion.
- ⊖ Traditional nature: Loss of the traditional nature of the sport, e.g., start times being changed to suit the media.
- ⊖ Adverts: Viewing experience may be interrupted by sponsors' adverts.
- ⊖ Tickets: Tickets can be difficult to obtain and expensive when they are available owing to an increase in popularity.
- ⊖ Merchandise: Sponsors may drive up the cost of merchandise.
- ⊖ Subscriptions: Viewers may have to pay to watch televised sport.

Sponsor / company

Corporate hospitality boxes.

- ⊕ Profit: Increased profit due to brand exposure and better sales.
- ⊕ Client experience: Gain free tickets to entertain clients at events.
- ⊕ Taxation: Sponsorship can be used to reduce the sponsor's tax bill.
- ⊖ Reputation: Impacted by negative publicity if a scandal happens in the sport that they sponsor.
- ⊖ Cost: Sponsorship can be very expensive and the sponsor may be legally tied in to continue sponsorship for a fixed period.
- ⊖ Supply and demand: If demand for products or services increases significantly, the company may find it hard to supply everyone.

Remember to focus on two things when answering questions about this topic: Firstly, which group is being asked about e.g., officials, and secondly, is the examiner asking for positives, negatives or for both?

It is common for students to write their answers about only the positive effects on performers even when the question is not asking for that.

Some points can be expressed as positives OR as negatives.

For example, an increased profile in the media may be what the performer hopes for or they may see it as adding to their pressure.

POSITIVE AND NEGATIVE IMPACTS OF TECHNOLOGY

Positives

Performer

- Fairness: Decisions are more accurate and fairer for performers.
- Performance: Standards of performance can improve through the use of equipment / analysis / rehabilitation etc.
- Analysis of performance: Allows for performance adjustments.
- Rehabilitation: Performers can use ice baths and other rehabilitation methods to recover more quickly.
- Safety: Advancements in helmets, for example, help to prevent injury.

Sport

- Analysis: Pundits analyse performance and educate viewers.
- Accuracy: People will trust that the sport is fair as decisions are more reliable.
- Design of equipment: Better equipment and clothing allow for higher standards of performance in the sport / more broken records.
- Facilities: The performance areas and viewing experiences are better.
- Spectators: Greater numbers in attendance with improved facilities.

Officials

- Decisions: Fairer decisions made that can be watched in slow-motion, e.g., **VAR** in football.
- Communication: Officials can easily communicate with each other.
- Proven to be right: Technology can show that officials were correct in their initial decision making.

Audience / spectator

- Action replays: Spectators can see the action from different angles, or in slow-motion.
- Analysis and education: Spectators can learn more about the sport from different angles, and statistics can be provided.
- 24/7 access: Spectators can gain information about performers, teams or clubs at all times of the day.
- Excitement: Technology can generate excitement by watching decisions being made, e.g. **Hawkeye** at the Wimbledon tennis championships.

Sponsor / company

- Exposure: Sponsors' brands can easily be advertised.
- Media mix: Different technological methods can be used to advertise, e.g. radio, TV graphics overlays, scoreboard messages, or a printed kit.
- Positive association: Sponsors can be linked to popular technologies.

Performer

- ⊖ Disruption: Waiting for on-field decisions disrupts performers' rhythm.
- ⊖ Punishment: There may be an increase in performers being punished through increased use of technology.
- ⊖ Cost: Pressure to use the most up to date equipment can be expensive.
- ⊖ Accessibility: Technology is not available equally for all performers, for example, some may not have analysis software available.

Sport

- ⊖ Officiating: Reduced trust in officials due to incorrect decisions.
- ⊖ Reliance: It may be perceived that the sport is over-reliant on technology.
- ⊖ Traditions: Some traditional aspects of the sport are lost.
- ⊖ Cost: The sport needs to find the money to make use of the most up to date technology.

Officials

- ⊖ Incorrect decisions: An official's initial decision can prove to be wrong.
- ⊖ Reputation: An official's reputation can be tarnished because of technological intervention in decision making.
- ⊖ Training: Officials need additional training in how and when to use technology.

Audience / spectator

- ⊖ Tradition: Spectators may prefer the traditional version of the sport, without technological intervention.
- ⊖ Delays: Spectators may not welcome the delays in play whilst technology is used to make decisions.
- ⊖ Cost: Expensive to buy the same technology used by the professionals.

Sponsor / company

- ⊖ Cost: Sponsored equipment may be expensive.
- ⊖ Cost: Keeping up with rival companies / teams who supply / use sponsored equipment.
- ⊖ Suitability: Sponsors' equipment might not suit the performer.

1. Describe **two** positive impacts of technology for the sponsor of a sporting event. [2]
2. Describe **two** negative impacts of technology for officials. [2]

1. *Any two from: The sponsor's brand can be advertised using technology.[1] There are different technologies that a sponsor could use to show their brand, e.g. TV, radio, shirt advertising, scoreboards.[1] The sponsor may get positively linked to technology that is popular with the public, e.g. Television Match Official (TMO) in rugby union.[1]*

2. *Any two from: The official's decisions may prove to be incorrect after the use of technology.[1] An official's reputation can be damaged.[1] Officials need to learn how to use the technology.[1]*

CONDUCT OF PERFORMERS

Sport should be played in the manner it is intended. Bending or breaking the rules can have serious consequences for performers and the reputation of their sport.

Etiquette

Etiquette is a convention or unwritten rule in an activity. It is not an enforceable rule, but it is usually observed.

In tennis, it is good etiquette to wait to serve whilst your opponent is getting ready to receive the serve. The sport of golf provides many good examples of etiquette, where there are many unwritten rules that performers observe, for example standing still and not walking across 'the line' of someone else's putt on the green.

Gamesmanship

Gamesmanship means attempting to gain an advantage by bending or stretching the rules to the limit. However, it is not breaking the rules.

Examples include shielding the ball in the corner of a football field to waste time, or challenging a line judge's call in tennis to disrupt the momentum of your opponent.

Sportsmanship

Sportsmanship means **fair play**, conforming to the rules, spirit and etiquette of the sport. Examples include shaking hands, kicking a ball out of play if a player is injured, and accepting the decision of umpires, officials or referees.

Contract to compete

The **contract to compete** is an unwritten agreement to follow and abide by the written and unwritten rules of the activity. This includes sportsmanship and etiquette.

The contract to compete as an unwritten agreement is seen when rugby union players respect a referee's decision and when shaking hands with the opposition. It is particularly relevant to Olympic and Paralympic athletes who take an oath to try their hardest, respect other competitors and do so without taking illegal performance-enhancing drugs.

PROHIBITED SUBSTANCES

Performance-enhancing drugs (PEDs) are substances that are designed to improve performance. They are often prohibited (banned), and when taken, break the contract to compete.

Remember that drugs can be addictive (as a negative side-effect).

Stimulants

- ✚ Increase alertness
- ✚ Reduce tiredness
- ✚ Increase aggression
- ✚ Speed up parts of the body, for example a 100m sprinter will react and move more quickly out of the blocks

- ➖ Cause high blood pressure
- ➖ Increase chance of strokes, heart and liver problems
- ➖ Increase the likelihood of performing with an injury

Narcotic analgesics

- ✚ Mask pain to continue performing, even when injured

- ➖ Lower blood pressure
- ➖ Lower concentration, leading to coma
- ➖ Cause constipation
- ➖ Create a temptation to compete whilst injured

Anabolic agents

- ✚ Increase rate and amount of muscle growth
- ✚ Allow you to train harder
- ✚ Speed up recovery
- ✚ Increase aggression and competitiveness

- ➖ Cause a hormonal imbalance
- ➖ Raise blood pressure
- ➖ Damage the liver, kidneys and heart

Peptide hormones (Erythropoietin - EPO)

- ✚ Increase in red blood cell count
- ✚ Improve oxygen carrying capacity
- ✚ Increase muscle growth

- ➖ Increase the viscosity (thicken) the blood
- ➖ Increase stress on the heart
- ➖ Increase risk of stroke

Diuretics

- ✚ Cause rapid weight loss
- ✚ Dilute the presence of illegal substances
- ✚ Remove excessive fluid

- ➖ Cause dehydration
- ➖ Lower blood pressure
- ➖ Cause muscle cramps

You are required to know the name, positive effects and negative side-effects of each type of PED.

You do not need to learn examples of each PED type.

Give **one** visible effect of taking anabolic agents. [1]

Positive effect: increased muscle mass.[1] Negative effect (caused by a hormonal imbalance): shrinking testicles / deeper female voice / increased female body hair / smaller breasts.[1]

PROHIBITED METHODS (BLOOD DOPING)

Blood doping involves the use of techniques or substances to increase a performer's red blood cell (RBC) count.

The process of blood doping

1 Blood is removed from an athlete several weeks before competition.

2 The blood is frozen.

3 The body makes more red blood cells to replace the ones that have been removed.

4 1–2 days before competition, the frozen blood is thawed and injected back into the performer, thus increasing their red blood cell count.

5 The performer now has more red blood cells which increases their oxygen carrying capacity and aerobic performance.

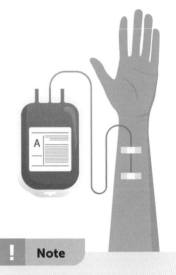

> **! Note**
>
> Caution! Blood doping comes with many negative side effects: thickening of the blood (viscosity), potential infection, potential for heart attack, and an embolism (blockage of a blood vessel).

Suggest why cardiovascular endurance may be improved by using the prohibited method of blood doping.
Justify your answer with a sporting example.　[4]

Cardiovascular endurance can only be improved with training as well.[1] Example: long-distance athletes.[1] Justification: Two from: to increase red blood cell count[1] so their oxygen carrying capacity in the blood in increased.[1] Improves the efficiency of the aerobic system.[1] Maintains performance without fatigue / excess lactic acid.[1]

DRUGS SUBJECT TO CERTAIN RESTRICTIONS (BETA-BLOCKERS)

Beta blockers can be prescribed by a medical practitioner but are subject to restrictions. Not everyone can simply take them at their own free will.

Effect of beta blockers

Beta blockers help to reduce heart rate, muscle tension and blood pressure, keeping a performer calm. They can reduce the effect of adrenaline, lowering arousal and improving focus; an unfair advantage in sports that require fine motor skills such as shooting, archery and golf.

However, they can have serious **side effects** including nausea, heart problems and weakness.

Beta blockers are not prohibited as such. They are simply restricted as some athletes may be given them by a medical practitioner.

It is common to be asked why beta blockers would be taken, what side effects they can have and what type of athlete would be likely to take them.

Discuss the positive effects and side-effects of taking beta-blockers.   [3]

Max two positives and two side-effects. Positives from: Reduce heart rate / muscle tension / blood pressure.[1] Reduce the effects of adrenaline.[1] Improve fine control / precision.[1] Negative side-effects from: Nausea.[1] Weakness.[1] Heart problems.[1] Tiredness.[1] Poor circulation.[1]

TYPES OF PERFORMERS THAT MAY USE DIFFERENT TYPES OF PEDs

Stimulants

Increase alertness.

A **sprinter** may take stimulants to be alert in the blocks.

Blood doping

Increases increases oxygen carrying capacity.

Endurance athletes have been known to use blood doping to enhance the efficiency of their aerobic system.

Anabolic agents

Increase muscle mass.

Any athlete requiring power and strength may take anabolic steroids e.g, a **discus thrower**.

Peptide hormones (EPO)

Increases oxygen carrying capacity.

Road cyclists may take peptide hormones to improve aerobic performance.

Beta-blockers

Increase fine motor control.

Archers may take beta blockers to enhance concentration and precision.

Diuretics

For weight loss.

Boxers or **jockeys** may take diuretics to make a weight category.

Narcotic analgesics

Relieve pain from over-training.

Narcotic analgesics allow injured athletes in **any sport** to continue training or competing.

THE ADVANTAGES AND DISADVANTAGES FOR PERFORMERS OF TAKING PEDs

In the pursuit of success, sports performers may turn to illegal drugs to enhance their performance and give themselves an unfair advantage over other competitors.

Why sports performers use drugs

Performance enhancing drugs are taken for a wide range of reasons. Many performers think they will never get caught and can get away with it. Others may be under considerable pressure from coaches to take drugs, to perform better or to 'win at all costs'. Further reasons include:

- Potential fame for winning
- For increased wealth / income
- To increase their chance of success / status / influence
- To 'level the playing field' in the belief that all other athletes are taking PEDs
- For a physiological benefit, for example to get stronger or faster.

Negative impacts on performers of taking PEDs

- Found out to be cheating / immoral
- Negative associated health risks
- Fined for taking PEDs
- Banned from competition / sport
- Reputational damage as a 'drug cheat'
- Loss of sponsorship or endorsement.

 Discuss questions usually mean that the examiner expects you to make a balanced judgement with the key points for each side.

Discuss the impact of taking anabolic steroids on a sprinter and their performance. [4]

Sprinters can gain an advantage through increased muscle mass which will increase their power, allowing them to run faster.[1] Steroids increase aggression and competitiveness which is an advantage in explosive events such as the 100 metres.[1] Winning could increase a sprinter's level of fame / income / sponsorship.[1]

Being caught would irreparably damage their reputation.[1] They would likely be removed from the team.[1] They may be banned from the sport.[1] A fine is commonly imposed which they would need to pay.[1] Sponsors are likely to drop their support immediately.[1] The performer may become addicted / could suffer health problems.[1]

THE DISADVANTAGES TO SPORTS OR EVENTS OF PERFORMERS TAKING PEDs

The reputation of an event, entire sport or sporting body rests on the actions of individuals within it.

The impact on sport

- The reputation of a sport could be heavily damaged if many competitors are found to be cheating by using drugs.
- The sports body could lose their key sponsorship leading to a loss of income.
- Spectator numbers and the overall fan base may decline, reducing interest, media coverage and income from ticketing and merchandise.
- Participation levels may fall if performers perceive that success is only possible with performance enhancing drugs.
- People may lose trust in past and future results.
- There would need to be a difficult, awkward and embarrassing process to revisit previous results so that medals and awards could be redistributed to fair performers.
- More funding would need to be invested into drug testing instead of helping emerging or elite athletes to perform to higher standards.
- Honest or 'clean' athletes can lose credibility if they are suspected or assumed to be drug users.

US Athlete Marion Jones admitted to taking steroids in the Sydney Olympics. She was stripped of her medals and banned from the Beijing Games.	North Korean Shooter Kim Jong-Su was expelled from the Beijing Olympic village after testing positive for beta blockers.	Romanian footballer Adrian Mutu was found to have taken stimulants so faced a nine month ban and around €17m in damages.

There are no real positive outcomes for a sport or event from performers taking PEDs. Focus on the negatives.

SPECTATOR BEHAVIOUR

Spectator behaviour at sporting events can have positive and negative effects.

Positive effects of spectator behaviour

⊕ Creation of **atmosphere** at the event
⊕ Creation of a **home field advantage** for the home team or an individual who is performing at their home venue
⊕ Increased **revenue** from merchandise and food sales
⊕ Spectators cause the **profile** of the sport to grow
⊕ Spectators can give performers additional **motivation**

Negative effects of spectator behaviour

⊖ Increased **pressure** on performers to do well
⊖ Increased potential for crowd trouble or **hooliganism**
⊖ **Safety costs** for police, security services and CCTV
⊖ Poor spectator behaviour may be **copied** by younger supporters or **put others off** attending or playing
⊖ Sport may suffer **reputational damage** due to poor spectator behaviour

The table below shows the attendance figures of six Premier League association football clubs in the 2022–23 season.

Average attendance

		Average attendance
1	Manchester United	73,742
2	West Ham United	62,456
3	Tottenham Hotspur	61,669
4	Arsenal	60,189
5	Liverpool	53,225
6	Manchester City	53,219

Analyse the data in the table to discuss the likely positive and negative impact of spectator behaviour on Manchester United football club. [4]

Max 2 marks for positives (must reference highest or largest once): Highest attendance so potential for biggest atmosphere.[1] Performers may be motivated by large fan base.[1] Highest potential revenue from ticket, food and merchandising sales.[1] Creation of larger home-field advantage.[1]

Max 2 marks for negatives: Highest attendance figure so greatest chance of hooliganism.[1] Highest security costs.[1] Highest chance of reputational damage.[1] Increased pressure of performers in front of large crowd.[1]

HOOLIGANISM

Hooliganism is disorderly, aggressive and often violent behaviour by spectators at sporting events.

Reasons why hooliganism occurs

1. **Rivalries** between teams, countries or areas.
2. **Hype** as the event is 'built up' in the media.
3. **Alcohol** or drugs may fuel aggressive behaviour.
4. Alcohol or drugs may **lessen inhibitions** causing people to behave in a manner they would not normally adopt.
5. **Gang culture** causes some people to act tribally, protecting their local area.
6. **Frustration** at players' performance or the decision of officials.
7. **Display of masculinity** to prove themselves to others.

1. Explain why alcohol and rivalry may lead to hooliganism at football matches. [2]

   1. *One mark for explanation of alcohol and one mark for explanation of rivalry. Alcohol: may lessen inhibitions which could cause someone to behave differently to normal.[1] Rivalry: Sense of pride and tradition to defend a team or territory.[1] Bragging rights.[1] History of aggression or violence between two groups.[1]*

Try to make acronym for some of the reasons for hooliganism e.g. **HARM** (**H**ype, **A**lcohol, **R**ivalry, **M**asculinity).

Strategies employed to combat hooliganism and control spectator behaviour

 Early kick off

As matches start earlier, supporters have had less time to drink excessive amounts of alcohol. However, this can mean less revenue for local pubs and a higher chance of hooliganism later in the day.

 Segregation of fans

Successful strategy to keep fans apart inside stadia but hooliganism has now moved away from the stadium so that hooligans can avoid being tracked by CCTV.

 Travel restrictions and banning orders

Known hooligans can be prevented from travelling internationally by having their passports confiscated. Banned individuals are placed on a watch list but this costs police time and money.

Hooligans who try to ignore their ban know they still need to be caught for it to be enforced. They may also have tickets bought for them by others.

 All-seater stadia

Seating controls the movement of spectators making it harder to mix with oppositions fans. Clubs promoted to higher leagues may be forced to install seating at their own significant cost.

 Improved security

CCTV, police and stewards can watch hooligans but it is an expensive way to track known culprits.

 Alcohol restrictions

Restrictions on sales inside and outside stadia reduce drunken and disorderly behaviour but lessen revenue for sales outlets. Local pubs may be forced to close. Fans may still drink at home causing issues later.

 Sharing of intelligence

At a heavy cost, police can share intelligence about the whereabouts, activity and likely intentions of hooligans.

 Education

Promotional campaigns and high-profile endorsements help to lessen the influence of hooligans or racists. The 'Kick it out' campaign is helping to educate everyone (even hooligans) that discrimination in sport is not acceptable.

---

2. Identify **three** strategies used to combat hooliganism. [3]

2. Any three from: Alcohol restrictions.[1] Early kick offs.[1] Banning / travel orders.[1] Intelligence sharing.[1] Segregation.[1] All seater stadia.[1] Security measures - police / stewards / CCTV.[1]

You should be prepared to evaluate the strategies used to combat hooliganism.

EXAMINATION PRACTICE 6

01   Which **one** of the following is **not** a type of sponsorship?   [1]
  ☐ A – Clothing
  ☐ B – Facilities
  ☐ C – Financial
  ☐ D – Social media

02   Which **one** of the following would be most effective at reducing heart rate?   [1]
  ☐ A – Anabolic steroids
  ☐ B – Beta blockers
  ☐ C – Diuretics
  ☐ D – Narcotic analgesics

03   Discuss the positive and negative effects of commercialised activity on a sponsor.   [4]

04   The use of performance enhancing drugs (PEDs) impacts performers and sport in general.

04.1 Explain how each of following prohibited PEDs may provide an advantage for performers.
      Justify each answer with a sporting example.   [4]
      Diuretics: _____
      Anabolic steroids: _____

04.2 Discuss the impact on the sport of boxing if performers are regularly found to be taking
      performance enhancing drugs.   [5]

05   State **three** types of media.   [3]

06   Participation in sport by those with a disability is around 20% lower than that of able-bodied adults.
     Evaluate the impact of **three** different factors in encouraging an increase in participation for
     disabled performers.   [9]

07   Sponsors may force performers to use equipment with the sponsor's name on it.
     Describe **one** other negative effect of sponsorship for a performer.   [1]

08   Sportsmanship and gamesmanship exist in sport.
08.1 Give **two** sporting examples of sportsmanship.   [2]
08.2 Give **one** reason for gamesmanship in sport.   [1]

09   Discuss the impact of technology on performers and spectators of sport.   [6]

10   Give **two** negative influences of spectators at sporting events.
     Provide a strategy to combat each one.   [4]

PHYSICAL, EMOTIONAL AND SOCIAL HEALTH, FITNESS AND WELLBEING

Each component of **wellbeing** is positively impacted by participation in sporting activities. They form part of a set to keep you healthy; each element working in conjunction with the others.

Physical health and wellbeing

Physical health and wellbeing is defined as having all body systems working well, and being free from illness and injury with the ability to carry out everyday tasks.

Physical health:

- improves heart function
- improves the efficiency of the body's systems
- reduces the risk of illness, e.g. diabetes
- means people are able to do everyday tasks without tiring
- helps to avoid obesity.

Mental health and wellbeing

Mental health and wellbeing is defined by the World Health Organisation (WHO) as a state in which every individual can realise their own potential; they can cope with the normal stresses of life; they can work productively and fruitfully, and they are able to make a contribution to their community.

Mental health:

- reduces stress, tension and anxiety
- helps with the release of feel good hormones (serotonin)
- increases confidence and self-esteem
- helps to alleviate depression
- helps people to control their emotions, such as anger.

⟷

Social health and wellbeing

Social health and wellbeing mean that basic human needs are being met (for example, food, shelter and clothing). The individual has friendship and support, some value in society, is socially active and has little stress in social circumstances.

Social health:

- provides opportunities to socialise and make friends
- enables cooperation and teamwork
- ensures people have the essential human needs (food, shelter, clothing).

Fitness

See **page 29** for more on the relationship between health and fitness.

Fitness is defined as the ability to meet/cope with the demands of the environment. Participation in physical activity can improve fitness, reduce the overall chance of injury and improve the ability to work, for example a manual labouring job or one that requires being on your feet all day.

THE CONSEQUENCES OF A SEDENTARY LIFESTYLE

Our **lifestyle** is the way in which we choose to live. This includes our choices over what to consume, how often to exercise and our decisions for employment. A **sedentary lifestyle** is one with irregular or no physical activity.

Consequences of a sedentary lifestyle

A sedentary lifestyle can involve spending long periods in front of the TV or sitting at a desk. Possible consequences of a sedentary lifestyle include:

Physical health

- Weight gain or obesity
- Heart disease
- Hypertension (high blood pressure)
- Diabetes
- Poor sleep

Mental health

- Poor self-esteem
- Lethargy

Social health

- Fewer opportunities to socialise

Explain **two** ways in which a sedentary lifestyle can impact physical health and wellbeing. [4]

A lack of exercise can result in consuming more calories than are burned through exercise,[1] leading to weight gain.[1] If the heart does not get exercise, it gets weaker and has to work harder / fatty deposits can build up in the arteries,[1] leading to hypertension / heart disease.[1] A lack of exercise can cause muscle cells to lose their sensitivity to insulin,[1] causing diabetes.[1] Exercise helps to prevent insomnia / reduces stress[1] to improve sleep.[1]

Hypertension (or high blood pressure) is defined as having an average systolic pressure of over 135.

OBESITY AND PERFORMANCE

Obesity is defined as having a **body mass index (BMI)** of over 30 or over 20% above standard weight for height ratio. Obese people have a high fat content, caused by an imbalance of calories consumed to energy expenditure.

How obesity may affect performance in physical activity and sport

Obesity:
- limits stamina/cardiovascular endurance
- limits flexibility
- limits agility
- limits speed/power.

Negative impacts on physical, mental and social health

Physical health
- Cancer
- Heart disease/heart attacks
- Diabetes
- High cholesterol

Mental health
- Depression
- Loss of confidence
- Anxiety
- Stress

Social health
- Inability to socialise
- Reluctant to leave home (if they are ashamed or embarrassed of their body).

BMI (Body Mass Index) is not on the specification, but it provides a rough approximation of obesity. Use the chart below to calculate your BMI.

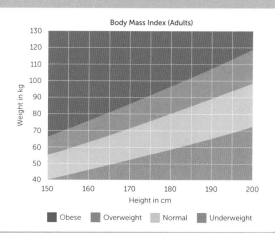

Body Mass Index (Adults)

Weight in kg / Height in cm

Obese Overweight Normal Underweight

Explain **two** ways that obesity could negatively impact performance in football or rugby. [2]

Limits stamina/cardiovascular endurance so a player cannot complete an entire game.[1] Limits flexibility so reduces the ability to reach/control a ball.[1] Limits agility so a player is less able to change direction/sidestep to avoid an opponent. [1] Limits speed/power so a player is less able to keep up with the ball / more likely to get tackled / cannot leap high enough to head the ball or in a line-out.[1]

SOMATOTYPES

Somatotyping is a method of classifying body type. A sport or sporting position (e.g. prop forward or winger) may be more suited to an individual with a particular type.

Endomorph

An **endomorph** is characterised by a **pear-shaped body**, with **some fatness**. Individuals commonly have **wide hips** and **narrow shoulders**. Sports or positions they are most suited to include discus, shot put, power lifting and forward rugby positions.

Endomorphs use their bulk to their advantage, to push forwards or to generate power. A higher fat content means they would find endurance sports more difficult, and less height makes racket sports, netball, volleyball and basketball more challenging.

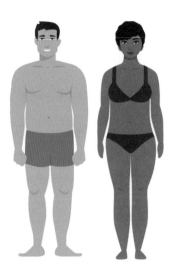 

Mesomorph

A **mesomorph** is characterised by a **muscular appearance**. Individuals typically have **wide shoulders** and **narrow hips**. They are ideally suited to football, swimming, sprinting and backline rugby positions.

Mesomorphs have powerful, athletic builds, providing bursts of anaerobic power combined with aerobic endurance. High muscle mass helps them to overcome opponents and withstand tackles, for example, in rugby. A wedge-shaped body helps them to pump their arms faster to generate a faster leg movement, creating speed.

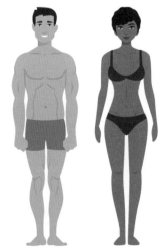 

Ectomorph

An **ectomorph** is characterised by being **tall** and **thin**. Individuals have **narrow shoulders** and **narrow hips**.

They are most suited to racket sports, high jump or endurance sports such as marathon running.

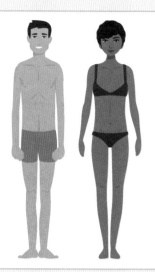

Justify why an ectomorph is well suited to distance running. [2]

They are thin and lightweight,[1] meaning they have less to carry over a long distance.[1] Longer legs[1] mean that their stride will be longer, helping them cover more ground in less time than those with typically shorter legs.[1] Narrow shoulders and hips[1] create less air resistance so they can slip through the air more easily, increasing speed.[1]

ENERGY USE

Energy is measured in **calories** (Kcal) and is obtained from the food we eat.

Calorie intake

The average adult male requires 2,500 Kcal/day and the average adult female requires 2,000 Kcal/day but this is dependent upon:

- **Age** – People under 25 need more calories. As you age, your body replaces muscle with fat and fat burns fewer calories.
- **Gender** – The average male needs roughly 25% more calories than females.
- **Height** – Taller people need more calories to fuel a larger frame.
- **Energy expenditure** (exercise) – Exercise burns calories which need to be replaced.

There are roughly 7700 Kcals in a kilo of fat.

In a simplified scenario, having a calorie deficit of 7700 or burning an additional 7700 calories over time will therefore result in weight loss of 1 kg.

Members of a community sports team charted their calorie intake over one week. Their average daily intake was calculated as shown below.

	Captain	Player 1	Player 2	Player 3	Player 4	Player 5
Average calories per day	2300	2000	2400	2500	2600	1800
Gender	Male	Female	Male	Male	Male	Female
Age	24	22	46	31	32	28
Height	205 cm	160 cm	170 cm	175 cm	170 cm	170 cm

(a) Analyse the data in the table. Identify which player is eating above the recommended calorie intake. [1]

(b) Explain **two** reasons why the captain may have been losing body mass. [4]

(a) *Player 4.[1]*

(b) *He is male and should be eating 2500 calories per day[1] so is short by 200 calories.[1] He is under 25[1] so will need more than the average 2500 per day.[1] Taller people need greater calories[1] so he should be eating slightly above the 2500 average.[1] He is an active member of a sports team so may be burning additional calories through exercise[1] that are not being replaced.[1]*

DIET

A **balanced diet** requires lots of different types of food to provide the right nutrients, vitamins and minerals required by your body.

A balanced diet

A balanced diet is defined as eating the right type and the right amount of food that your body requires, consuming only as many calories as your body burns each day. Excess calories are stored as fat. A calorie deficit can cause a reduction of body mass through fat and muscle loss.

Increasing the amount of exercise you do, will require an increase in calories and nutrients, for example, additional protein to help muscle growth.

The reasons for a balanced diet

| 1 | The body needs sufficient calorific energy available for its activity. |

| 2 | The body needs the correct nutrients for growth and hydration. |

| 3 | Consuming too much can create unused, or surplus, energy which is stored as fat. This could cause obesity (particularly with excess saturated fat). |

| 4 | To make sure that we get the right vitamins and minerals to strengthen bones, fight infection and release energy from food. |

Rickets is caused by a lack of vitamin D and calcium affecting bone development or weakening bones in adults.

Scurvy is caused by a lack of vitamin C, causing tiredness, joint pain and bleeding gums.

State why it is important to eat a wide range of food types. [1]

You cannot get all the nutrients you need from a single food source.[1]

NUTRITION

Nutrition is defined as the intake of food, considered in relation to the body's dietary needs. Good nutrition involves a well-balanced diet, combined with regular physical activity.

The role of carbohydrates, fat, protein and vitamins or minerals

A balanced diet contains roughly 55–60% carbohydrate, 25–30% fat, 15–20% protein.

This can come from eating a variety of fruits and vegetables; bread, rice and pasta; meat, fish and eggs; and milk and dairy products.

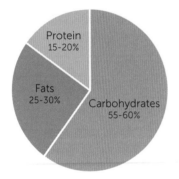

 You do not need to know about specific vitamins and minerals.

 Carbohydrates

Carbohydrates are the main and preferred **energy** source for all types of exercise, of all intensities.

 Fat

Fats are essential for the body, though some types are better than others. Fat provides more **energy** than carbohydrates but only at low intensity, for example walking or jogging. Fat helps to **insulate** the body, it protects vital organs with additional **cushioning** and supports **cell growth**.

 Protein

Protein is required for **growth and repair** of muscle tissue, developing muscular strength.

Vitamins

Vitamins and minerals, such as calcium, are for maintaining the efficient working of the body systems and for general health.

1. Explain why a sprinter needs plenty of carbohydrates and protein in their diet. [4]
2. Give **one** health risk as a result of consuming more than the recommended 25–30% fat. [1]

1. *Carbohydrates are burned at varying intensities, unlike fat, so their bodies can break down the carbohydrates into glucose for increased energy during intense training and competition.[1] Carbohydrates would therefore be the preferred energy source of the body.[1] Protein helps to develop muscular strength so they can increase their power and race times.[1] Outside training and competition, the muscles require protein to repair themselves.[1]*
2. *Heart disease,[1] high cholesterol,[1] hypertension (high blood pressure caused by a narrowing of the arteries).[1]*

REASONS FOR MAINTAINING WATER BALANCE

People need to have enough water for their bodies to function normally. **Dehydration** refers to an excessive loss of body water, interrupting the function of the body. Rehydrating means to consume water to restore correct levels.

Consequences of dehydration

 Blood will thicken (increase in viscosity) with less water content, which slows blood flow, meaning less oxygen is supplied to the working muscles and to the brain. It also means that waste products such as CO_2 and lactic acid cannot be removed as efficiently.

 The heart will have to work harder, as a result of blood thickening, to supply oxygen to the working muscles during exercise. It may also develop an irregular rhythm. This could result in a poorer performance for a sports person.

 The body could increase in temperature (overheat) causing dizziness or fainting. This could prevent a performer from continuing their training or activity.

 Reaction times slow down as the brain is receiving less oxygen and muscles get tired. This can result in poor decision making and reduced skill levels.

 Muscles will tire, causing cramps, a limited range of movement and potentially preventing activity from continuing.

A sprinter of the Bahamas pulled up with cramp in the Women's 200m semi-final of the IAAF World Championships at The Khalifa International Stadium, Doha, Qatar.

(a) Give **one** cause of cramp. [1]

(b) Explain how the sprinter may have adjusted her water intake for the championships in the hot, dry climate in Qatar. [1]

(a) *Dehydration / tired muscles / insufficient oxygen to the working muscles.[1]*

(b) *Increase water intake[1] in order to compensate for increased loss of water through sweating / increased evaporation in the breath.[1]*

EXAMINATION PRACTICE 7

01   Which **one** of the following is a benefit of mental health and wellbeing? [1]

☐ A – Improved heart function

☐ B – More able to complete everyday tasks

☐ C – Reduced risk of physical illness

☐ D – Reduced stress

02   Mina is a 32-year-old female with a sedentary lifestyle.

Which **one** of the following is the most suitable daily calorie intake for her to maintain her body mass? [1]

☐ A – 1900

☐ B – 2100

☐ C – 2400

☐ D – 2500

03   How much protein should a balanced diet contain? [1]

☐ A – 5–10%

☐ B – 15–20%

☐ C – 25–30%

☐ D – 55–60%

04   Identify the somatotype of the rugby prop shown in figure 1. [1]

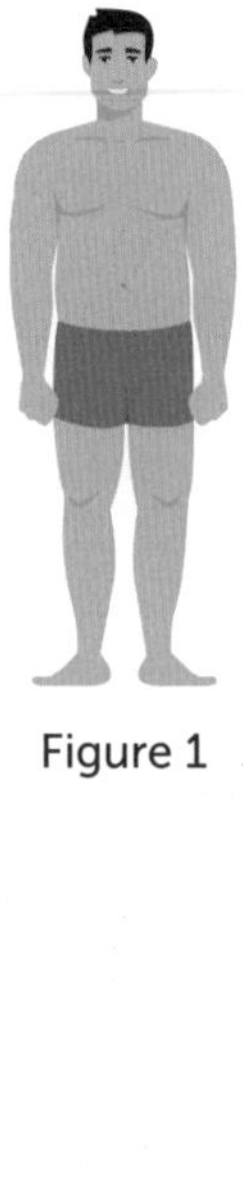

Figure 1

☐ A – Ectomorph

☐ B – Endomorph

☐ C – Mesomorph

☐ D – Plastomorph

05   Participating in sports improves social health and well being.

05.1 Define social health and wellbeing. [1]

05.2 State **two** positive effects that being physically active can have on social health and wellbeing. [2]

06   Table 1 shows the body mass index (BMI) scores of five adults.

	Adult 1	Adult 2	Adult 3	Adult 4	Adult 5
BMI Score	17	21	26	35	28

Table 1

06.1   Identify which adult would be classified as obese.   [1]

06.2   Obesity can cause social, physical and mental ill health.
       Give **one** way in which obesity can negatively impact mental health.   [1]

06.3   State **one** way in which a person's body fat percentage can be reduced.   [1]

	Jan	Feb	Mar	Apr	May	Jun
BMI Score	28	26	25	24	23.5	23

Table 2

Adult 5 has decided to reduce their BMI. Table 2 shows their progress over 6 months.

06.4   Plot the BMI points onto the graph below and draw a line between them showing the trend.
       Label the axes.   [2]

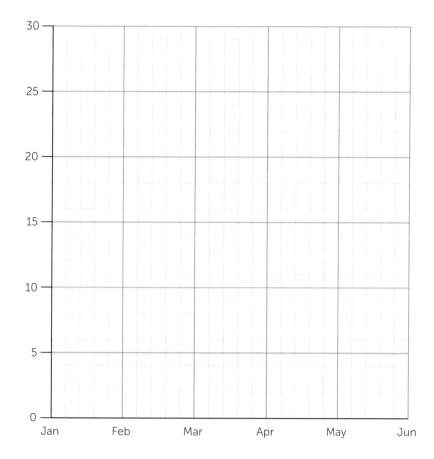

07   Oscar has used somatotyping to classify himself as an ectomorph.

07.1   Give **two** characteristics of an ectomorph.   [1]

07.2   Oscar is training for a county high jump event.
       Discuss whether being an ectomorph provides Oscar with a competitive advantage.   [6]

08   Give **one** reason for a balanced diet.   [1]

09   During his 21-day Tour de France race, Chris Froome reportedly consumed 8000 calories per day.

       Explain **one** reason why performers may need to increase their calorific intake.   [2]

10   Explain how dehydration may impact the heart and blood flow of a performer.   [2]

NON-EXAM ASSESSMENT (NEA)
Practical performance in physical activity and sport

Information about the non-examined assessment:

Assessed by teachers
100 marks
40% of the qualification grade

1.   Performance assessment (practical performance) – 75 marks

For each of three sporting activities, students will be assessed in skills in progressive drills (10 marks per activity) and in the full context (15 marks per activity).

The three activities that you choose must come from the lists below and should include:

- A team activity,
- An individual activity, **and**
- Any other activity of your choice

Team sports:
Acrobatic gymnastics, association football, badminton, basketball, camogie, cricket, dance, figure skating, futsal, Gaelic football, handball, hockey, hurling, ice hockey, inline roller hockey, lacrosse, netball, rowing, rugby league, rugby union, sailing, sculling, squash, table tennis, tennis, volleyball, water polo.

Specialist sports: blind cricket, goalball, powerchair football, table cricket, wheelchair basketball, wheelchair rugby.

Individual sports:
Amateur boxing, athletics, badminton, canoeing / kayaking (slalom or sprint), cycling, dance, diving, equestrian, figure skating, golf, gymnastics, rock climbing, sailing, sculling, skiing, snowboarding, squash, swimming, table tennis, tennis, trampoline, windsurfing.

Specialist sports: Boccia, polybat.

2.   Performance analysis assessment (analysis and evaluation) – 25 marks

Students will be assessed on their analysis (15 marks) and evaluation (10 marks) of performance to bring about improvement in one activity.

PERFORMANCE ASSESSMENT: PRACTICAL PERFORMANCE

Your non-examined assessment requires you to take part in **three** different activities, evidencing specific skills and your performance in the full context of each sport.

Guidance notes

Part 1   Skills

Each of the activities have a list of skills that should be performed. Most activities have five skills in the list.

- All skills must be evidenced.
- Skills must be seen in progressive practices that get harder.
- The progressive practices should incorporate a suitable level of challenge.
- The progressive practices should incorporate an element of competition, but not into the full context version.

If a skill starts in a static drill that is relatively easy, it should progress quickly. You will need to make sure that you are suitably challenged so may need some suitably challenging opponents.

For example, the skill of passing in netball should incorporate all the different variations, i.e. chest, shoulder, one-handed and two-handed.

Evidence of this might include:

- Static passes.
- Passes on the move.
- Passes under pressure.
- Conditioned passes under competitive pressure in a set space.

> **! Note**
>
> Evidence in your three sports can be presented live or via audio/video evidence. However, it is important to structure your evidence correctly.

Part 2   Full context

Sports must be assessed in the full context, competitive version of the activity, for example, 7-a-side netball, or 11-a-side association football. One of the most important aspects is to show yourself being challenged so this is often achieved by performing at the highest standard that you can.

A few additional points to consider include:

- You do not need to play in several different positions in team games.
- You can submit video performances to evidence what standard you are at, but the evidence must be unedited, i.e., continuous footage.
- You can use multiple halves or quarters e.g., a half of rugby from one game and a different half from another.
- The evidence should be appropriately officiated.
- The length of the evidence is up to you. A minimum recommendation is usually one half in team sports, a set of tennis, a game of badminton, 9 holes of golf for example.

> Look at the relevant page in the specification for more detail relevant to your chosen activity, for example, dance should be in front of an audience.

PERFORMANCE ANALYSIS ASSESSMENT: ANALYSIS AND EVALUATION

Your analysis and evaluation coursework can be written (typed) or completed as an interview.

Most students will type their coursework and analyse their own performance in an activity they have chosen to show practically. However, it can be written about another person who has performed in a sport that is included in the list in the specification.

Analysis: Strengths and weaknesses

When completing this work, it is advised that you title each section to make it clear. For example, in the analysis section, you are likely to title the following areas:

> Fitness component: Strength
> Fitness component: Weakness
> Skill or technique: Strength
> Skill or technique: Weakness

The fitness components are listed on **pages 30 to 31** of this guide.

The skills and techniques are listed in the specification under your chosen activity criteria.

For each strength and / or weakness, start off by making it clear what it is, for example *"My fitness weakness is ..."*.

You can then produce a short paragraph that explains why that **fitness component** is relevant to your chosen sporting activity.

The rest, and the biggest part, of each strength (or weakness) is about justifying why you have highlighted that strength (or weakness) based on **two** recent performances. This should be written in **past tense** as the performances have already happened. For your fitness strength for example, you should explain why it was a fitness strength in **two** recent performances. If you only refer to one recent performance, you will not gain as high a mark.

For each strength or weakness, think about:

- Who were you competing against?
- What was happening in the performance?
- When was the strength or weakness revealed?
- Why was it a strength or a weakness? What impact did it have on the performance?

Consider the **impact** that the strength or weakness had on you as a performer and on your overall performance.

Note

For each strength and weakness, the recent performances you refer to can be different or could come from the same performances – it's up to you.

Evaluation: The use of theoretical principles to cause improvement

When you start your evaluation section, don't forget to title it as the Evaluation.

The whole of the evaluation needs to be personalised and should not be general. It is about **you** and what you will do and therefore the whole section should be in the **future tense**.

Sections of the evaluation

1

It is suggested that your first sub-title is:
Training type to improve my fitness weakness

In this section you should choose **one** suitable training type to use to improve your fitness weakness. You need to explain what the training type is and why it would help your fitness weakness, but you also need to:

- Justify why this training type is right for you, and
- Justify why it suits what's available to you and / or what you can fit into your weekly schedule.

2

It is then suggested that your next sub-title is: **My session**

In this section you should outline what a **single** session of training will involve for **you**. It must be personalised, and not general, so must be designed by you, for you. It should be written in the future tense as it is a plan for future improvement.

Think about:

- What's available to you and how you will carry it out?
- How will you warm up?
- What exercises you will do and why you are you doing them?

You will also need to specify an **intensity level** that you will achieve in your training session. The intensity level should be calculated, but it should also be justified, i.e., why is that level of intensity correct for you? You may also detail how you would apply the SPORT and FITT principles if the session was to continue on to other sessions, but you do not need to write up any future sessions.

3

It is suggested that the final title is: **Theoretical area to eradicate my skill weakness**

In this section you must choose one aspect of the theory course (not a training type) that could be applied for you to improve on your skill weakness (not your fitness weakness). Whatever you choose, you must show:

- You fully understand what the theory is
- In future tense, how it would apply it to you
- How it will be used to remedy your skill weakness

EXAMINATION PRACTICE ANSWERS

01   A – Femur.   [1]

02   D – The movement of the arm away from the midline of the body.   [1]

03   B – Right atrium → right ventricle → left atrium → left ventricle.   [1]

04   C – Increased heart rate.   [1]

05   Support [1], protection of vital organs by flat bones [1], movement [1], to provide a structural shape [1], provide points for muscular attachment [1], for mineral storage [1] and blood cell production. [1]   [3]

06.1 Ligaments are less elastic than tendons. [1] Ligaments connect bone to bone / tendons connects bone to muscle. [1] Ligaments provide support and stability to a joint whereas tendons are designed to move the bone at a joint. [1]   [2]
06.2 Small fluid filled sacs used to cushion parts of a joint / reduce friction between moving parts within the joint.   [1]

07.1 An isotonic concentric contraction [1] of the tricep. [1] Do not accept isotonic without concentric.   [2]

07.2 The muscles are contracting but not changing length / there is no movement created by the contracting muscles [1] as the position is/forces are constant. [1]   [2]

07.3 Example responses may include a handstand, hold in a deadlift, hold at the top of a pull-up, crucifix in gymnastics rings or pushing in a scrum. Award one mark for any suitable answer.   [1]

08.1 Muscles are attached to bones by tendons. [1] When muscles contract, they pull on the tendon, which moves the bone. [1] Muscles work in antagonistic pairs. [1] As one contracts, the other relaxes. [1] Bones create lever systems which can be moved. [1]   [3]

08.2 X: Tidal volume (mL) [1], Y: Residual volume (mL).[1]   [2]

08.3   [2]

08.4 Cardiac output = stroke volume x heart rate
      0.07 × 170 = 11.9 litres. [1] Award 1 additional mark for correct conversion to litres.   [2]

08.5 Pectoral (muscles) [1] / sternocleidomastoid [1].   [1]

08.6 Diastole means that the muscle of the heart chambers relaxes to enable filling.[1] Systole means that they are contracting / emptying / ejecting the blood (pumping).[1]   [2]

09   This question should be marked in accordance with the levels-based mark scheme on **page 117**.   [6]

      Indicative content may include:
      AO1: Knowledge of the effects on the body of long-term fitness e.g:
      • Body fat will be reduced over time.
      • Weight may be reduced.
      • Improved muscle strength.
      • Improved muscular endurance.
      • Improved speed.
      • Improved suppleness / flexibility.
      • Improved stamina.
      • Increase in the size of the heart (hypertrophy).
      • Lower resting heart rate (bradycardia).

AO2: Application to an ice skater e.g:
- Reducing body fat/ weight will help with lifts, jumps and lessen the impact on landing.
- Increased muscle mass in the legs will help with explosive power for jumps.
- Suppleness and flexibility can help with the spin positions required.
- Increased stamina can help a skater avoid fatigue before the end of their performance.

AO3: The importance of long-term fitness training to an ice skater e.g:
- Lifts and jumps are a core part of a skater's routine so weight and strength need to be maintained.
- Performances can be improved through increased training, tailored to their needs so they maintain and increase their performance scores.
- A dip in fitness may result in a dip in performance scores so a regular training programme in preseason, competition season and post season needs to be put in place
- Variety is important to avoid boredom
- They may need dietary supplements to increase carbohydrate intake which converts into glucose for energy, protein to help build and repair muscle (hypertrophy), fluids and salts for hydration and effective body function
- SPORT and FITT need to be applied to ensure a safe and effective training program. Overload should be reached but not overdone.

10   Oxygen consumed.   [1]

01.1   Class 1 lever / 1st class lever / first order lever.   [1]

01.2   Diagram must be labelled. Accept load/resistance.   [2]

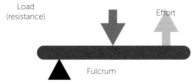

02.1   Plane – Sagittal. [1] Axis – Transverse. [1]   [2]

02.2   Plane – Transverse. [1] Axis – Longitudinal. [1]   [2]

02.3   Extension.   [1]

02.4   Effort arm is always shorter than resistance arm. / It has a short effort arm. / MA = effort arm / resistance (load). [1]
       Lever has low strength to effort ratio. [1] Lever is inefficient when considering strength. [1]
       3rd class levers allow a load to be moved more quickly / over a greater distance. [1] Third class levers always have an
       MA of less than 1. [1]   [2]

02.5   Movement of the limbs (arms) away from the midline of the body. [1] Movement of the arms to the side [1] for balance. [1]

01   A – Agile.   [1]

02   B – Motor racing.   [1]

03   B – Progressive overload.   [1]

04   B – 204.   [1]

05   Improved mental health / self-esteem / appearance / reduced depression [1] could improve the desire to train or exercise
       (in public). [1]
       Improved blood pressure / diet / quitting smoking [1] could make exercise easier to approach / more enjoyable /
       more manageable. [1]
       Improved friendship groups / social standing / reduced loneliness [1] may provide greater desire / opportunities to
       train socially. [1]   [2]

06.1   Flexibility. [1]
       - Increases muscular elasticity which reduces chance of injury / decreases DOMS. [1]
       - Limbs have a greater range of movement so they can reach more shots / improve their technique. [1]
       - Flexibility improves balance and mobility, keeping the player responsive / on their feet. [1]

- Cardiovascular endurance. [1]
- Increases the duration that they are able to perform at their peak for with a raised heart rate. [1]
- Muscular endurance. [1]
- Avoids fatigue in muscles used repeatedly throughout a match. [1]
- Speed. [1]
- Helps a player to reach shots on the other side of the court / aids position between shots to return to the centre of the court. [1]   [2]

06.2 Definition, 1 mark: The ability to move two or more body parts together smoothly and efficiently. [1]
Importance, up to 3 marks: Hand eye coordination is required when hitting the ball. [1]
The player must align their body with the incoming shot and position themself to strike with power. [1]
The racket should hit the ball in the sweet spot so that they get maximum power on the ball. [1]
To hit a ball on the move. [1]
The player must move into the right position on the court to hit the ball before the ball reaches that point. [1]
Better coordination should result in more shot points awarded / fewer unforced errors, providing a competitive advantage. [1]
A serve must be coordinated to toss the ball up and hit it perfectly. [1]   [4]

07   David's score indicates that he has average agility. [1]
Elizabeth's score indicates that she has good agility. [1]
Even though David performed the test faster than Elizabeth, as a male, he is expected to be faster [1] / the scores compensate for males and females so Elizabeth is grouped in a higher performance category. [1]   [3]

08.1 Use the handgrip dynamometer in the dominant hand. [1] Squeeze the handle with maximum effort. [1]
Keep the elbow at 90 degrees. [1] Keep the arm close to the body. [1] Record the best score. [1]   [3]

08.2 This question should be marked in accordance with the levels-based mark scheme on **page 117**.   [6]
Indicative content may include:

AO1: Knowledge of the grip test e.g:
- The test measure grip strength.
- The test does not measure the strength of any other muscle group.

AO2: Application to a rock climber and a kayaker e.g:
- A rock climber needs a strong hands and grip in order to hold on to a rock face.
- A kayaker does not need a very strong grip, other than to hold onto the paddle.
- The test is a standard test to measure grip strength with national benchmarks.

AO3: The importance of the test to a rock climber and a kayaker e.g:
- Grip strength is a fundamental skill for rock climbing as climbers need to use hand holds.
- A kayaker needs to be able to hold on to the paddle, but there are far more important muscle groups such as the arms and back that depend more on strength in kayaking.
- The test does, to some extent, replicate the movements of a rock climber using hand holds. It does not replicate the movements of kayaking.
- Grip strength dynamometers may measure grip more in the whole hand rather than just the strength of the fingertips to cling onto a rock, so it may be limited as a measure of climbing ability.
- Grip strength is a poor indicator of ability for a kayaker since it does not evaluate their overall strength, but it may provide some indication of general fitness and strength.
- There are other standardised tests that may be better for both rock climbers and kayakers such as a sit-up bleep test or a wall toss test to measure muscular endurance and coordination.

09

Component of fitness	Method
Power	Lift high weights, quickly
Muscular strength	Lift high weights, few times
Muscular endurance	Lift low weights, many times

10.1 Three from: Avoid over training [1], wear appropriate clothing and footwear [1], apply taping/bracing as necessary [1], maintain good hydration [1], use the correct technique [1], allow for recovery with appropriate rest in between sessions [1].   [3]

10.2 This question should be marked in accordance with the levels-based mark scheme on **page 117**.   [9]
Marks for this question: AO1 = 2, AO2 = 2, AO3 = 5
Indicative content may include:

AO1: Knowledge of plyometric training and other factors e.g.

- Plyometric training involves jumping, bounding and hopping
- It is good at developing power / explosive strength, but also speed
- Training involves creating an eccentric contraction of a muscle which moves straight into a larger concentric contraction to maximise the length of the contraction and the power of the muscle movement
- Diet may improve performance alongside any types of training
- The principles of SPORT and FITT should be applied, regardless of the type of training
- Callum should plan his warm-ups, rest periods and recovery.

AO2: Application to Callum e.g.

- Plyometric training can improve Callum's muscular endurance
- Plyometric training can improve Callum's power
- Plyometric training can improve Callum's speed
- Power will be needed to avoid or quickly dodge an opponent
- Callum will need a high level of fitness before starting plyometric training as it exerts high forces on muscles which could tear if he isn't already strong as there is a high risk of injury
- If Callum adopts plyometric training during the football playing season, an injury could mean he misses the remaining fixtures
- Callum would not need any specialist equipment and could practice plyometrics almost anywhere
- He may need dietary supplements to increase his carbohydrate intake to convert this into glucose for energy, protein to help build and repair muscle (hypertrophy), fluids and salts for hydration and effective body function
- SPORT and FITT need to be applied to ensure a safe and effective training program. Overload should be reached but not over done
- Recovery practices should be put into place to reduce DOMS and prevent injury or tightness.

AO3: Evaluation of the appropriateness of plyometrics and other factors to Callum e.g.

- Plyometric training is well suited to improving speed and power in the legs which is a desirable attribute in a football player
- Football players needs speed when running for/with the ball so increased leg power will improve this fitness component for Callum
- Football players need explosive power in the legs to be able to respond to potential tackles, shoot or jump to head the ball so more powerful legs will help to improve the power and accuracy of a shot, improve height from a standing jump and improve the speed of response to avoid a tackle or fallen player.
- Training can be tailored to Callum to ensure that it is suitable for his current level of fitness and strength and that he has sufficient recovery time before the next match
- In a full match, other training methods may replicate the sporting movements of football more closely or provide greater benefits to Callum
- Callum could also combine plyometric training with other types of training to work on his cardiovascular (aerobic) endurance, core stability and agility such as interval training and circuit training to provide benefits of both aerobic and anaerobic exercise which reflects the stop/start nature of football and the bursts of energy required when a player prepares to get on the ball / gets the ball
- Ice baths, massages and a planned cool down routine including stretches will help reduce DOMS and aid a faster recovery before the next match/training session
- Training should reflect the SPORT and FITT principles so that it is specific to Callum's needs, so that progress overload is reached and to avoid tedium.

Accept any other relevant points.

11.1   Anaerobic activities do not use oxygen [1] so changing the amount of available oxygen has little effect on the muscles. [1] Anaerobic activities are generally bursts of only 60 seconds so altitude training will not have any significant benefit in lengthening the duration of bursts. [1]   [2]

11.2   High altitude training puts athletes in an oxygen deprived environment so that their bodies are forced to produce more red blood cells [1] to carry an equivalent amount of oxygen around the body. [1] When the athlete moves to a lower altitude, the additional blood cells can now carry more oxygen [1] providing the muscles with increased supply [1] so that the athlete can sustain higher levels of intense activity for longer periods. [1] Delays fatigue. [1] Reduces lactic acid production. [1]   [4]

12   Warming up prepares your body for activity by speeding up your cardiovascular system. [1] Increased blood flow loosens the joints [1] and provides greater flow of oxygen to the muscles. [1] Stretching prepares muscles for physical stress and improves the range of movement. [1]   [2]

01   C – The Austrian skier looks uncomfortable at the moment.   [1]

02.1 Correctly labelled x axis (Season/Year) and correctly labelled y axis (Number of yellow cards). [1] Bars correctly plotted for each season. [1]   [2]

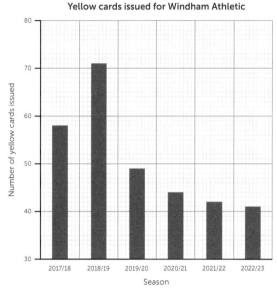

Yellow cards issued for Windham Athletic

02.2 Data for 2018/19 (71) was much higher than other data points and outside of the trend.   [1]

02.3 Yellow cards generally decreased over the six year period.   [1]

02.4 Two from: Change of manager with stricter policies on foul play. [1] Change in FA regulations. [1] Club incentives for players to reduce bookings. [1] Change in referee(s). [1] Change in playing style and technique. [1] Greater fitness / ability of players. [1] Greater team bonding and morale. [1] Accept any other reasonable response.   [2]

02.5 Accept between 38 and 41.   [1]

01   A – Feedback about the technique used.   [1]

02   A – Having your body mass moved over the downhill ski by an instructor.   [1]

03   A – Jumping a hurdle in sprinting.   [1]

04   C – Shoulder barge in football.   [1]

05   B – Shy.   [1]

06   Sailing. [1] The environment is constantly changing (wind / current / waves) which the performer needs to make adjustments for. [1] The performer needs to respond to movements by opponent boats in order to outwit them / make counter movements. [1] Movements are performed differently depending on which direction the boat is facing / aiming to go. [1]
      Rugby tackle. [1] The performer needs to change their approach depending on the situation. [1] The performer needs to outwit their opponents with changes to their direction/strategy/pace depending on the state of play. [1] The game environment is constantly changing. [1]
      Accept other suitable examples and justifications. Maximum one mark for the example.   [3]

07.1 As a beginner, Jo could be demotivated by unrealistic outcome goals. [1] Jo may not be motivated to be the best at this stage, just to be the best she can be. [1] Jo needs to focus on her own skills rather than those of others to improve. [1] Performance goals cannot be affected by others, so they are more likely to be achieved by a beginner. [1]   [2]

07.2 Accepted – Jo needs to have agreed the target of 15%. [1] Realistic – 15% may be too low / difficult to achieve depending on the time frame she has to achieve this. [1] Time bound – Provide a definitive date by which she must achieve the target. [1] It is already specific and measurable.   [2]

08.1 Labels in order: Decision-making [1], Output [1], Feedback. [1] [3]

08.2 A performer gathers information from the display / environment via their senses, for example, in golf, the wind speed and direction, hazards and the distance to the pin in a drive. [1]

They choose what information is relevant to them, blocking out all other information, for example birdlife, other players, spectators [1] and apply it to short term memory.

Explanations must relate to a sporting example. [2]

09.1 Marks for correct x axis labels [1], correct y axis labels [1], correct shape of the graph [1], correct placement of the graph towards the high arousal end. [1] [4]

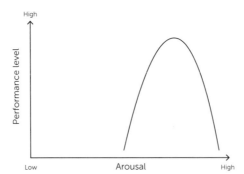

09.2 Mental rehearsal [1] which involves envisaging the actions of a skill. [1]

Imagery and visualisation [1] is a relaxation technique used by performers to picture themselves in a calm environment or with positive outcomes. [1]

Deep breathing [1] which involves exaggerated inhalation and exhalation. [1]

Positive self-talk [1] which involves a performer giving themselves instruction in their head. [1] [2]

10 Intrinsic motivation comes from within the performer, so they can always feel a sense of achievement with progress. [1] Extrinsic factors are likely to be medals in elite championships which can only be won by very few performers. The rest need internal motivation to keep pushing / keep going. [1] Intrinsic motivation may be used as a tool to reach their extrinsic goal, [1] but provides a way to keep putting in continued effort every day. [1] At an elite level, extrinsic factors may be the main motivation left as they have so much time and effort to reach that goal, so intrinsic factors have less importance. [1] [4]

Paper 2, Topic 2

01 D – Social media. [1]

02 B – Beta blockers. [1]

03 Positives: Any two from: Profit - increased profit due to brand exposure / selling more product. [1] Client experience - gain tickets to entertainment clients at events. [1] Taxation - sponsorship can be used to reduce the sponsor's tax bill. [1]

Negatives: Any two from: Reputation - sponsor may gain negative publicity if a scandal happens in the sport that they sponsor. [1] Cost - sponsorship can be very expensive and the sponsor may be legally tied in to continue sponsorship for a period. [1] Supply / demand - if demand for products / services increases significantly, the company may find it hard to meet the demand. [1] [4]

04.1 Diuretics: Any activity that has a weight category – e.g., horse racing, judo, boxing etc. [1] Justification: Diuretics allow you to reduce your weight. [1] Reduction in weight can allow a 'performance criteria' to be met. [1]

Anabolic steroids: Any activity that requires strength or power – e.g., rugby union, sprinting, discus, shot etc. [1] Justification: Steroids can increase muscle mass to produce strength. [1] Steroids can allow you to train harder to make greater gains. [1] Steroids can help you to speed up recovery to train more. [1] Steroids can help to increase aggression / competitiveness, e.g., in a rugby tackle. [1] [4]

04.2 The reputation of boxing and boxers could be heavily damaged. [1] People may lose trust in past and future results. [1] The sports body could lose their key sponsorship leading to a loss of income. [1] Spectator numbers and the overall fan base may reduce, reducing interest, media coverage and income from ticketing and merchandise. [1] Participation levels may fall if grass roots performers perceive that success is only possible with performance enhancing drugs. [1] There would need to be a difficult, awkward and embarrassing process to revisit previous results so that belts and titles could be redistributed to fair performers. [1] More funding would need to be invested into drug testing instead of helping emerging or elite athletes to perform to higher standards. [1] Honest or 'clean' athletes can lose credibility if they are suspected or assumed to drug users. [1] [5]

05 Any three from: Television, [1] radio, [1] printed press, [1] internet, [1] social media. [1] [3]

06   This question should be marked in accordance with the levels-based mark scheme provided on page 117.   [9]

Indicative content

AO1 - Potential factors

Familiarisation with activities available; access; cultural change; subsidies; role models; socio-economic circumstances; role models; stereotyping; media coverage etc.

AO2 - Application to disabled performers

Access: as some sports facilities do not cater for the accessibility requirements of all disabilities, access could be improved. Role models: There is a need for more specific disabled role models in the media. Subsidies: Disabled performers could receive subsidies towards transport or membership or access to a sports facility. Stereotyping: There may be a stereotype that disabled users are unable to participate.

AO3 - Evaluation of the factors

Ramps for wheelchairs would allow more wheelchair users to access facilities. Targeted campaigns in the media could highlight disabled role models, inspiring others to take part. Those of a low socio-economic circumstance may be able to afford to participate if subsidies for transport and for access are put in place. Promotion and education about disabled sports may help to break stereotypes and start a culture that all people, irrespective of ability can participate.

Accept any other suitable response that evaluates factors promoting disabled participation.

07   Any one from: The sponsor may demand that the performer attends sponsors events. [1] The performer may get attached to a brand name that they do not like. [1] The sponsor may demand a certain level of performance to maintain sponsorship. [1] The performer may become reliant on the sponsor's money and equipment. [1]   [1]

08.1   Two from: Be friendly to all competitors and avoid unpleasantness. [1] Take measures to reduce the risk of injury to others. [1] Help injured players before playing on. [1] Promote their sport in a positive way and be a positive role model. [1] Accept the decision of umpires, referees and officials. [1] Accept any other valid example.   [2]

08.2   To increase the likelihood of winning / to turn the game around if losing. [1] To gain fame / financial reward for winning. [1] To feel clever by 'playing' the rules to their letter. [1] Copying the behaviour of others. [1] Frustration of losing a point / being in a losing position. [1] Orders from the coach. [1]   [1]

09   This question should be marked in accordance with the levels-based mark scheme on page 117.   [6]

AO1 Knowledge of technology: Technology assists with decisions, enhancing performance, analysis, rehabilitation and safety.

AO2/AO3 Balanced discussion of the impact of technology on performers and spectators:
Performers may feel that the sport is fairer with technology making decisions. Their performance may increase through using more advanced equipment which may give them more opportunity to break records. Technology can help provide detailed analysis of performance / biomechanics as feedback / better extrinsic knowledge of performance. Speed of recovery may be improved through advances in medical technologies / ice bath research / hypoxic tents. Safety advances in protective sportswear decrease the chance / severity of injury.

Performers may feel that their momentum or rhythm is disrupted by additional time waiting for technology to assist in officials' decision. Technology may see more than officials so player behaviour may be punished more frequently. The cost on performers to have the very latest equipment in order to compete with others is increasing. Some players may not get access to the latest technology which puts them at a disadvantage.

Spectators commonly enjoy an action replay / or analysis from pundits / match stats as sports are in play / or as a sports roundup. Education is gained from screen overlays and analysis. Some technology can add excitement to a game, such as Hawk Eye in tennis or a photo finish in sprinting or horse riding. Coverage is available through various channels 24/7.
Spectators may prefer the tradition and rhythm of sports without interruptions form technology. Delays may detract from the game. Spectators inspired to take part in sports they enjoy watching may be discouraged by the cost of aspirational equipment used by their heroes.

10   Potential for crowd trouble / hooliganism, [1] can be combated by segregation of fans / early kick offs / alcohol restrictions / travel bans for known hooligans. [1] Safety costs and concerns [1] can be relieved through all-seater stadia / education on safety / behaviour for fans. [1] Declining participation numbers amongst younger performers who see other behaving poorly [1] can be tackled through education / promotional campaigns / high profile endorsements e.g. stop racism / improved safety / banning orders for trouble-makers. [1] Accept other valid responses.   [4]

Paper 2, Topic 3

01   D – Reduced stress.   [1]

02   A – 1900.   [1]

03   B – 15–20%   [1]

04   B – Endomorph.   [1]

05.1 Basic human needs are being met (food, shelter and clothing). The individual has friendship and support, some value in society, is socially active and has little stress in social circumstances. [1]

05.2 Two from: Opportunities to socialise with other people, [1] make friends, [1] enjoy some teamwork or team sports, [1] / cooperate with other people. [1] [2]

06.1 Adult 4. [1]

06.2 One from: Depression, [1] loss of confidence, [1], anxiety, [1] stress. [1] [1]

06.3 One from: Consume fewer calories. [1] Increase energy expenditure. [1] [1]

06.4 Award one mark for points correctly plotted on the graph. One for correctly labelled axes. [2]

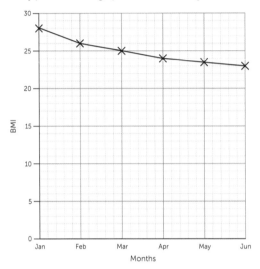

07.1 Two from: Tall, [1] thin, [1] narrow shoulders, [1] narrow hips. [1] [1]

07.2 This question should be marked in accordance with the levels-based mark scheme on page 117. [6]
Indicative content may include: [6]

AO1 Knowledge of ectomorphs e.g:
- Have long legs. Need flexibility and suppleness.
- Performers benefit from being lightweight.
- Ectomorph body fat will be low. Weight may be reduced.

AO2 Application to a long jumper e.g:
- Low body fat / weight will help with jumps and lessen the impact on landing.
- Low body weight will help increase jump height.
- Low muscle mass in the legs may not help with explosive power for jumps.
- Suppleness and flexibility can more easily be achieved without excess body fat.
- Long legs provide greater starting height for jumps.

AO3 The competitive advantage of an ectomorph in long jump e.g:
- Long legs provide greater leverage. Being taller helps jump over a higher bar.
- Lower body weight will reduce the load/resistance on take off.
- Other competitors who have larger body shapes may have to carry more weight over the bar.
- Being thinner/narrower helps to reduce the profile through the air, reducing wind resistance.
- Being thinner/narrower reduces the chance of catching the bar on the way over.
- More likely to be successful at long jump than a mesomorph / endomorph as they carry more bodyweight / are wider.

08 Unused energy is stored as fat, which could cause obesity, [1] suitable energy can be available for activity, [1] the body needs nutrients for energy, growth and hydration. [1] [1]

09 Sustained exercise burns a lot of energy [1] which needs to be replaced through increased calorific intake. [1] Additional nutrients / protein / sugars are required [1] to help fuel the body / repair muscles. [1] 2500 calories a day for men is recommended [1] but this should be increased according to the additional levels of activity undertaken. [1] [2]

10 The heart will have to work harder as the blood is more viscous [1] which results in less oxygen supply to the working muscles. [1] Blood flow will be slower as the blood is thicker [1] so less oxygen is supplied to the brain and working muscles, slowing decision making / reaction time / causing cramp. [1] Fewer waste products can be removed from the working muscles [1] as there is reduced blood flow. [1] Lowered blood oxygen levels can cause cramps [1] causing a performer to pull up / retire from activity. [1] [2]

LEVELS-BASED MARK SCHEME FOR EXTENDED RESPONSE QUESTIONS

What are extended response questions?

Extended response questions are usually worth 6 or 9 marks. These questions are likely to have command words such as 'compare', 'explain' or 'evaluate'. You need to write in continuous **prose** when you answer one of these questions. This means you must write in full sentences (rather than in bullet points), organised into paragraphs if necessary.

You may need to bring together skills, knowledge and understanding from two or more areas of the specification. To gain full marks, your answer needs to be logically organised, with ideas linked to give a sustained line of reasoning.

Marking

Calculations are **not** marked using 'levels of response' mark schemes, but written answers are marked this way. Examiners look for relevant points (indicative content) but they also use a best fit approach. This is based on your answer's overall quality and its fit to the descriptors for each level.

Example level descriptors

Level descriptors vary, depending on the question being asked. Level 3 is the highest level and Level 1 is the lowest level. No marks are awarded for an answer with no relevant content. The table gives examples of the typical features that examiners are asked to look for.

Level	6 Marks	9 Marks	Level descriptors
3	5–6	7–9	The answer is detailed, accurate and clear. A range of relevant points are linked logically. Application of knowledge to the scenario is appropriate. Most relevant data is used, if provided. Explanations show comprehensive understanding. A conclusion is well-reasoned, supported by a range of correct reasons and an appropriate use of terminology.
2	3–4	4–6	The answer is mostly detailed but not always clear. It includes some relevant points with an attempt at linking them logically. Some relevant data is used (if provided). Some logical explanation is provided. A conclusion is given that may not fully match the reasoning made. Terminology is used on occasions.
1	1–2	1–3	Relevant points are made. They are not logically linked and may be unclear. Little or no data is used. Only simple descriptions are made. If a conclusion is given, it may not match the reasoning given in the answer. Terminology is not used or is not appropriate.
0	0	0	No response or nothing worthy of credit.

INDEX

Symbols

1RM 36, 45
30 Metre Sprint Test 36

A

abdominal muscles 4, 12
abduction 6
ability 58
adduction 6
adrenaline 11
aerobic
  capacity 47
  exercise 14
  power 33
age 74
aggression 67
agility 30, 32
agonist 7
alveoli 8
anabolic agents 83, 86
anaerobic exercise 14
anaerobic power 35
ankle 2, 5, 6, 7, 24
antagonist 7
aorta 9
arousal 65, 66
arteries 9
atria 10
axes 26

B

balance 30, 32
ball and socket joints 5
bar charts 53, 54
basic skills 58
behaviour 89
beta-blockers 85, 86
biceps 4, 7
blood 9
  cells 3
  doping 84, 86
  flow 49, 101
  vessels 9
bone marrow 3
bones 2
bracing 46
bradycardia 17

C

breathing 12, 16
bronchi 8
bronchioles 8
bursae 5

calories 98
capillaries 9
carbohydrates 15, 100
cardiac
  cycle 10
  hypertrophy 17
  output 11
cardiovascular endurance 17,
    30, 33, 47
cartilage 5
cartwheels 26
chambers of the heart 10
charts 53, 54
chest 2
circuit training 39
circumduction 6, 23
closed skill 58
clothing 46
commercialisation 76
competitive season 48
complex skill 58
components of fitness 17, 30
concentric contraction 7
conduct of performers 82
continuous training 40
continuum 58
contractions 7
contract to compete 82
cool down 49
coordination 30, 33
cramp 16
cranium 2
cricket bowl 23, 58
culture 73

D

data 37, 52
deep breathing 66
dehydration 101
delayed onset muscle soreness
    (DOMS) 15, 16, 49

deltoid 4, 7
detraining 47
diaphragm 12
diastole 10
diet 15, 99
diffusion 8
direct aggression 67
disability 75
diuretics 83, 86
anabolic agents 83, 86
dorsiflexion 6, 24
dynamic strength 31

E

eccentric contraction 7
ectomorph 97
effort 20
effort arm 22
elbow 2, 5, 6, 7, 23
endomorph 96
endurance 17, 30
engagement patterns 72
erythropoietin (EPO) 83
etiquette 82
excess post-exercise oxygen
    consumption (EPOC) 15
exercise, effects of 16
exhalation 12
expiratory reserve volume 13
explosive strength 31, 35, 43
extension 6, 23, 24
externally-paced skill 58
extrinsic feedback 64
extrinsic motivation 69
extroverts 68

F

family 75
fartlek training 41
fat 100
fatigue 16
feedback on performance 64
femur 2
fibula 2
fine motor skills 58, 65, 68
first class lever 20, 22
fitness 29, 30, 93
fitness testing 37

FITT 38
flexibility 30, 34
flexion 6, 23, 24
forward roll 27
frontal plane 26
fulcrum 20

G

gamesmanship 82
gaseous exchange 8, 47
gastrocnemius 4, 7
gender 72
glucose 14, 15
gluteals 4, 7
glycogen 15
goal setting 59
graphs 53, 55
gross motor skills 58, 65, 68
guidance on performance 62

H

haemoglobin 8
hamstring groups 4
hamstrings 7
Handgrip Dynamometer Test 36
Hawkeye 80
head 2
health 29, 93, 95
heart 10
heart rate 11, 15, 16, 17, 44
high altitude training 47
high intensity interval training 42
hinge joints 5
hip 5, 7, 24
hip flexors 4, 7
hooliganism 89, 90
humerus 2
hydration 46
hypertension 94
hypertrophy 17

I

ice bath 15
ice skating 26
Illinois Agility Test 32
imagery 66
indirect aggression 67
information processing model 61
inhalation 12

injury prevention 46, 49
inspiratory reserve volume 13
intercostal muscles 12
interval training 42
Interviews 52
intrinsic feedback 64
intrinsic motivation 69
introverts 68
inverted-U theory 65
isometric contraction 7
isotonic contractions 7

J

joint capsule 5
joints 2, 3, 5

K

kicking 24
kinaesthetic feedback 64
knee 2, 5, 6, 7, 24
knowledge of performance 64
knowledge of results 64

L

lactic acid 14, 15, 49
latissimus dorsi 4, 7
lever systems 20
ligaments 5
light-headedness 16
line graphs 53, 55
load 20
load arm 22
longitudinal axis 26
lumen 9
lungs 8

M

manual guidance 63
massage 15
maximal strength 31, 36
measurements 37
mechanical advantage 22
mechanical guidance 63
media 76, 77, 78
mental health 93
mental rehearsal 66
mesomorph 96
minerals 3, 100
motivation 69

movement 3
Multi Stage Fitness Test 33
muscles 4, 7, 16, 49
muscular endurance 17, 30, 34

N

narcotic analgesics 83
nausea 16
negative feedback 64
nutrition 100

O

obesity 95
observations 52
one repetition maximum calculation 45
One Rep Max Test 36
open skill 58
outcome goals 59
overload 38
over training 46
oxygen debt 15
oxyhaemoglobin 8

P

patella 2
pathway of air 8
pathway of the blood 10
pectorals 4
peptide hormones 83, 86
performance 65
performance-enhancing drugs (PEDs) 83, 86, 87, 88
performance goals 59
physical assistance 63
pie charts 55
pivot 20
plane 26
plantar flexion 6
plantarflexion 24
plyometric training 43
positive feedback 64
post-season training 48
power 31, 35, 43
pre-season training 48
prime mover 7
principles of training 38
progressive overload 38
protein 100
push up 23

Q

quadriceps 4, 7
qualitative data 37, 52
quantitative data 37, 52
questionnaires 52

R

race 73
radius 2
reaction time 30, 35, 101
red blood cells 3, 47
rehydration 15, 16
religion 73
residual volume 13
resistance 20
rest 46
reversibility 38
ribs 2
rotation 6, 23
rotator cuff 4
Ruler Drop Test 35
running 24

S

sagittal axis 26
sagittal plane 26
scapula 2
seasonal training 48
second class lever 21, 22
sedentary lifestyle 94
self-paced skill 58
self-talk 66
shoulder 2, 5, 7
sidestepping 26
Sit and Reach Test 34
Sit-Up Bleep Test 34
skeleton 2
  functions of 3
skills 58

SMART targets 60
social grouping 72
social health 93
somatotypes 96
somersault 27
specificity 38
spectator behaviour 89
speed 17, 31, 36, 43
spine 2
spirometer trace 13
sponsorship 76, 77, 78
SPORT 38
sportsmanship 82
squats 25
stamina 17
standing vertical jump 25
static strength 31
static stretching 42, 46
stereotype 75
sternum 2
stimulants 83, 86
Stork Stand Test 32
strength 17, 31, 36
stress management 66
stretching 15, 46
stroke volume 11
suppleness 17
surveys 52
sweat 15, 16
synovial
  fluid 5
  joint 5
  membrane 5
systole 10

T

tabular data 54
talus 2
taping 46
technology 80

tedium 38
tendons 4, 5
third class lever 21, 22
throw in 20, 23
tibia 2
tibialis anterior 4, 7
tidal volume 13
trachea 8
training 39
  threshold 44
  zone 44
transverse axis 26
transverse plane 26
triceps 4, 7

U

ulna 2

V

valves of the heart 10
VAR 80
vasoconstriction 9
vasodilation 9
veins 9
ventricle 10
verbal guidance 62
vertebrae 2
Vertical Jump Test 35
visual guidance 62
visualisation 66
vitamins 100

W

Wall Toss Test 33
warm up 46, 49
water balance 101
weight training 43
well-being 29, 93
work:rest ratio 39

EXAMINATION TIPS

When you practice examination questions, work out your approximate grade using the following table. This table has been produced using a rounded average of past examination series for this GCSE. Be aware that boundaries vary by a few percentage points either side of those shown.

Grade	9	8	7	6	5	4	3	2	1	0
Boundary	77%	72%	67%	61%	57%	49%	37%	25%	13%	0%

1. Read questions carefully. This includes any information such as tables, diagrams and graphs.
2. Remember to cross out any work that you do not want to be marked.
3. Answer the question that is there, rather than the one you think should be there. In particular, make sure that your answer matches the command word in the question. For example, you need to recall something accurately in a **describe** question but not say why it happens. However, you do need to say why something happens in an **explain** question.
4. Use connective words in your answers, for example, 'because', 'such as', or 'so that' as these force you to give an explanation for your answer, commonly gaining an additional mark in questions worth two or more marks.
5. In questions where the command word is **discuss**, remember to give both sides of the argument.
6. In longer answer **analyse** or **evaluate** questions (6 or 9 marks), be sure to include AO1 (knowledge and understanding), AO2 (application of knowledge) and AO3 (analysis and / or evaluation). Give detailed reasons and focus on the impact in AO3.
7. Both the examination papers will include multiple-choice questions (MCQs). Make sure you neatly fill in the circle of the answer you want to be marked. If you change your mind, put a cross in the box (from corner to corner). If you change your mind back again, put a circle neatly around the box.
8. Show all the relevant working out in calculations. If you go wrong somewhere, you may still be awarded some marks if the working out is there. It is also much easier to check your answers if you can see your working out. Remember to give units when asked to do so.
9. Plot the points on graphs accurately and use a ruler. Ensure that you are drawing the type of graph asked for in the questions. Do not confuse bar charts with line graphs. Label all lever diagrams, graphs and charts fully - e.g. levers must have the symbols and the words - i.e. fulcrum and triangle.
10. Try not to confuse the pathway of air in the respiratory system with the process of gaseous exchange.
11. Write legibly! Candidates often lose marks where examiners are unable to read their handwriting.
12. Write your answers on the lines provided. If you need more space, use additional paper to complete this, clearly numbering the response with the question number. Make it clear that you have used extra paper in the answer space provided.

Good luck!

These guides are everything you need to ace your exams and beam with pride. Each topic is laid out in a beautifully illustrated format that is clear, approachable and as concise and simple as possible.

They have been expertly compiled and edited by subject specialists, highly experienced examiners, industry professionals and a good dollop of scientific research into what makes revision most effective. Past examination questions are essential to good preparation, improving understanding and confidence.

- Hundreds of marks worth of examination style questions
- Answers provided for all questions within the books
- Illustrated topics to improve memory and recall
- Specification references for every topic
- Examination tips and techniques
- Free Python solutions pack (CS Only)

Absolute clarity is the aim.

Explore the series and add to your collection at **www.clearrevise.com**

Available from all good book shops

amazon 𝕏 @pgonlinepub

New titles
coming soon!

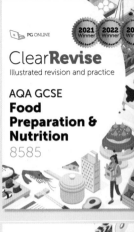

ClearRevise
Illustrated revision and practice

AQA GCSE
Food Preparation & Nutrition
8585

ClearRevise
Illustrated revision and practice

OCR
Creative iMedia
Levels 1/2
J834 (R093, R094)

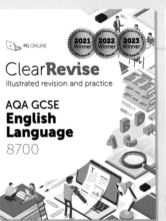

ClearRevise
Illustrated revision and practice

AQA GCSE
English Language
8700

ClearRevise
Illustrated revision and practice

Edexcel GCSE
History 1HI0
Weimar and Nazi Germany, 1918–39
Paper 3

ClearRevise
Illustrated revision and practice

AQA GCSE
Geography
8035

ClearRevise
Illustrated revision and practice

OCR GCSE
Computer Science
J277

ClearRevise
Illustrated revision and practice

AQA GCSE English Literature
An Inspector Calls
By J. B. Priestley
8702

ClearRevise
Illustrated revision and practice

Edexcel GCSE
Business
1BS0

ClearRevise
Illustrated revision and practice

AQA GCSE
Combined Science
Trilogy 8464
Foundation & Higher

ClearRevise
Illustrated revision and practice

AQA GCSE
Design and Technology
8552